THE AMATEUR

THE
AMATEUR

The Pleasures of Doing
What You Love

ANDY MERRIFIELD

V
VERSO
London • New York

First published by Verso 2017
© Andy Merrifield 2017

The moral rights of the authors have been asserted

1 3 5 7 9 10 8 6 4 2

Verso
UK: 6 Meard Street, London W1F 0EG
US: 20 Jay Street, Suite 1010, Brooklyn, NY 11201
versobooks.com

Verso is the imprint of New Left Books

ISBN-13: 978-1-78663-106-0 (HB)
ISBN-13: 978-1-78663-451-1 (EXPORT)
ISBN-13: 978-1-78663-108-4 (UK EBK)
ISBN-13: 978-1-78663-109-1 (US EBK)

British Library Cataloguing in Publication Data
A catalogue record for this book is available from the British Library

Library of Congress Cataloging-in-Publication Data

Names: Merrifield, Andy, author.
Title: The amateur : the pleasures of doing what you love / by Andy
  Merrifield.
Description: London ; New York : Verso, 2017.
Identifiers: LCCN 2016050506 | ISBN 9781786631060 (alk. paper)
Subjects: LCSH: Amateurism. | Self-culture. | Hobbies.
Classification: LCC GV14.45 .M44 2017 | DDC 306.4/87–dc23
LC record available at https://lccn.loc.gov/2016050506

Typeset in Fournier by MJ & N Gavan, Truro, Cornwall
Printed and bound by CPI Group (UK) Ltd, Croydon, CR0 4YY

'Our era of technicians makes abundant use of the nominalised adjective "professional": it seems to believe that therein lies some kind of guarantee.'

— Guy Debord

'"Experts", he muttered, smiling scornfully. Snatching up his top hat, he shook his head bitterly and went out.'

— Anton Chekhov

For Corinna & Lili-Rose,
painters outside the lines …

Contents

Preface: *Feeling 'More Alive'*   xi

1. Professionals and Amateurs   1
2. A Question of Faith   17
3. The Measure of Knowledge   39
4. City of Amateurs   63
5. Work in the Crystal Palace   89
6. Professional Democracy   117
7. The Genius of Curiosity   137
8. Hobby-Horse   151
9. The Amateur Revolution   171

Acknowledgements   205
Notes   207

Preface

Feeling 'More Alive'

Professionals are everywhere. Little gets done nowadays without a professional 'expert' offering their specially acquired knowledge: downscaling and evaluating, measuring and advising, scheming and sorting out life for millions of people the world over. It's as if everybody needs to get in on the act, to brand their whole personality as a compliant 'professional', to advance their career, to live a happy life. It's like we're being told there are only two types of people: professionals (including wannabe professionals) and losers.

In this book, I want to challenge this order of things. I want to present an alternative category, the nemesis to the professional expert: the *amateur*. Here the amateur is both a real and an imagined category – somebody who does exist today, but also someone who ought to exist. The amateur is a *normative* construct, a person who's lying latent in society, waiting to flourish. They're someone with an alternative sensibility, unwilling to fall for the expert scam, not feeling the need to sell themselves to the highest bidder. They're dedicated to doing things successfully and well yet without any great reward, sometimes without any reward at all.

In the accepted wisdom, we think of amateurs as people who dabble, who do things as a hobby rather than as a living, at weekends, in their spare time. They may be really good at something, 'experts' in their own right – at gardening, amateur dramatics, car mechanics – but it's still amusement, something *unimportant*. Professionals, by contrast, are those who apply themselves in *important*, instrumental ways. They're there to be listened to, taken seriously.

A staggering array of professional and expert bodies dominates our social, economic and political life. They preside over the implementation of social needs and the adjudication of public utility. Experts can be found at all levels of government and economic policy, in health systems and educational programmes. They formulate the algorithms of the business of science and write the language of the science of business. They oversee research and development and they squirrel away the benefits of patents and intellectual property rights. Consultants, advisors and think-tank wonks offer not-so-laissez-faire encouragement to our self-regulating, deeply undemocratic market system.

Professional experts instruct us about what we must learn and what we must read, what needs to be sold. They decide what aspects of public culture must to be written off, what benefits are without economic value, whose jobs are 'inefficient'. Experts assert how we must present ourselves in public, how we must itemise the parameters of our work, how we must talk, how we must write. They know best about investing our money, if we have any, how much tax we should pay, what our legal rights are. Experts even provide guidance to politicians about how they should govern. Experts model our personalities, validate our hopes and desires, advise us how to live and how to die.

It's not that all experts are necessarily wrong; it's more the mantle of power experts now assume, the degree to which they seem to rule unquestioned and supreme. Experts are both a new church and a new mafia, seducing and extorting at one and the same time, all the while equipped with their own irrational rationality of organisation, their largely unaccountable prowess.

In *The Amateur*, I want to intervene in the pervasive production, and acceptance, of this reality. I want to try to invent another reality, examine what amateurism means today and what it might mean. I shall do so by critiquing professionalism, staking out the fault lines that exist between amateurs and professionals, working through these fault lines *thematically*, shifting between personal identity and work relations, knowledge production and political power, technocratic representation and popular participation, urban studies and militant activism. I want to delve into the tensions between amateurs and professionals in each domain and show that these tectonic plates are, in fact, political divisions that can be reclaimed and moved.

Whenever I hear professional business types utter their marketing and management mantras, or professional academics talk about research assessments and finance, about grant money and committees, I feel the same sense of outsiderhood and stupefaction that Dostoevsky's Underground Man feels on attending a reunion of his old school friends. Unlike him, they're all 'successes', professionals who've amassed the rewards of status and commercial victories. But the Underground Man 'hates the harshly self-confident sound of their voices', and is struck by 'the pettiness of their thoughts, the stupidity of their pursuits, their games, their conversations'.[1]

They understand little about real life, he says, about 'the most essential things'. They never read books and 'have no interest in the most inspiring, impressive subjects'. They mistake rank for intelligence, and even at an early age were 'already thinking about snug positions'. They've grown to worship success and want it for themselves. 'Everything honourable, but humble and down-trodden', the Underground Man says, 'they greet with disgraceful and unfeeling laughter', including the Underground Man himself. Their demeanour is 'superficial', affecting 'an air of cynicism'. 'They blabber about excise duty, about business in the Senate, about salaries and promotions, about His Excellency, and the best means to please him, and so on, and so on.'

Ever since my late teens, when I first read Dostoevsky, I've identified with the Underground Man. At first it may have been because we were both frustrated clerks, ill-suited to what we were doing, or what we were supposed to be doing. He'd been a clerk for a while, in the Russian civil service; I was serving my time, in the late 1970s, as a wages clerk at the dock board in Liverpool, beholden to professional managers, to professional ways. We hit it off despite our epochal differences, despite our age gap and different tongues. Like him, I was rude and enjoyed being rude. It was all I could do for not taking bribes, for not wanting in. Later I was adrift, often between jobs – between tiresome, pointless office tasks, managed by professionals. Most people thought I was lucky to have any job at all, but I hated it. I was a self-avowed Underground Man.

Dostoevsky remains vital to me, and to this book, because he helps construct the amateur spirit. He affirms the idiosyncrasies of the outsider, the person who doesn't easily fit into established norms and desires. Dostoevsky wrenches apart two different paradigms for living: the career path versus the life journey. The Underground Man's old school chums have opted for the former, a trajectory not of risky fulfilment but of safe routine, not of defiance but of compliance. They've chosen a route towards preordained success, dominated by personal ambition and respect for authority, a desire to *be* authority. Theirs is a closed and closeted world; the Underground Man's vision is more open-ended, more uncertain, more adventurous in its self-affirmation and self-expression, full of existential suffering yet 'more alive'.

Today, from my observations and conversations, I can see that there are many people across the globe struggling to feel more alive, many *underground amateurs*, trying to shrug off professional clothing. Our sense of discomfort with the world of work and with the life of the world is there: we know it, we dread it. This book is for all those people trying to feel more alive, more engaged with what you do and how you do it. It's a struggle against professionalism and the structures of work, life and business that professionals now put in place. It's a struggle not to fit into a standardised mould. But it's something positive, too, a yearning to live more broadly and interestingly, to be curious and inquisitive, rather than smugly omniscient. To feel more alive is to reclaim the spirit of amateurism, in its different forms, and to counter the ideologically driven world of professionals.

All my adult life, I've been drawn to scholars and writers, wayward poets and square-peg novelists whom I call amateurs. They'll crop up in the pages ahead: not only Dostoevsky but also Hannah Arendt, Charles Baudelaire, Walter Benjamin, Marshall Berman, Guy Debord, Ivan Illich, Franz Kafka, Jane Jacobs, Karl Marx, Edward Said et al. In different ways and in different contexts, these thinkers all de-professionalised reality, in their lives and in their writings. They challenged box tickers, bean counters and rule followers, taking bold and courageous stances in the affirmation of independent thought. They voiced condemnation at the same time as they upheld certain passions and virtues about life, passions and virtues I admire, even love. They can help us rediscover the pleasures of doing what we love.

1

Professionals and Amateurs

My first brush with the professional world came early, when I was five years old. I didn't know it back then, but would piece it together later. It was 1965, the year my Nan was dispatched to Barons Hey at Cantril Farm, the brave new housing estate on the fringes of Liverpool. There were several problems with this dispatching. For one thing, my Nan, my granddad and their daughter (my aunt Emily) were relocated whether they liked it or not. They didn't get a choice in the matter, just a letter through the mail. The family was being moved on *for their own good*, as part of the 1960s mass slum clearance programme, shifting 15,000 people from inner-city Liverpool and exiling them to Knowsley, beyond the city limits. Their terrace house on Holden Street in Toxteth, off Upper Parliament Street – their prim and proper, if poor, little terrace house, on a block where everybody knew one another – was deemed squalid by urban 'experts'.

The professional planners had enough raw data to prove it. They had other big ideas then about what urban life should entail. The new project followed the 'Camus' system of building, the French engineer Raymond Camus's fully industrialised prefabricated construction technique, patented in 1948. Factory-manufactured concrete panels could be put up rapidly and cheaply, producing 2,000 units of housing a year. The French state adopted it for its low-and-moderate-income housing (HLM) stock, as did Le Corbusier in his upscale Unité d'habitation in Marseilles. Between 1950 and 1968, the technique inspired the Soviet Union in its massive state reconstruction programme.

Yet even before Cantril Farm was finished, it was falling apart. It was leaky and damp; there was no soundproofing between flats; communal corridors lacked lighting, and what there was often didn't work; lifts were broken and services non-existent. There was no public transport, no doctors' surgeries, no shops. It was a high-rise wilderness set in a wilderness, a fallow field in a fallow field, cut off from anywhere, from any memorable past and any discernible future. It was row upon row of grey, drab breeze-block towers, homes for 20,000 wounded denizens, mushrooming on land the council acquired at a bargain. Little wonder my Nan didn't last very long in this wilderness. She died a few years later of a broken heart, within a broken community. Nor did my aunt thrive there, dying soon after my Nan at the age of thirty-eight. At five, I knew nothing; later I heard words that describe this death-form: *alienation*, *alienated life*, usually instigated by nameless, faceless professionals.

Two decades later, after I first read Marshall Berman's *All That Is Solid Melts into Air*, I recognised how my Nan and granddad were like the old couple he talks about so wonderfully: Philemon and Baucis from Goethe's *Faust*, *Part Two*. (I didn't know it then but Marshall, who died in 2013, would become a dear friend and inspirational amateur.) The couple became a drag on the whims of progress as defined by professionals. Philemon and Baucis, like my Nan and granddad, were pawns in a bigger story, dispensable and movable on the chessboard of modern 'development'.[1]

Master builder Faust becomes obsessed with redeveloping an area of land around the coast. He dreams of making a whole new society there. But a problem arises. A small parcel is occupied by Philemon and Baucis, whose cottage looks out over the dunes. The sweet couple offer aid and hospitality to shipwrecked sailors and wanderers. Yet Faust wants rid of them and their world. He offers them money. But they refuse to move. At their age, what would they do with money anyway? And where to go, after living there so long? 'That aged couple should have yielded', Faust curses. 'I want their lindens in my grip,/ Since these few trees that are denied me/ Undo my worldwide ownership.'[2] Faust wants the old couple out of the way, but doesn't want to do it himself, nor to know the details of how it's done.

So Mephistopheles, Faust's darker spirit, steps in one night and kills the old folk. 'Faust contracted out the dirty work of development', Marshall writes, 'and then washes his hands of the job, disavowing the jobber once the work was done.' Two centuries on, the hand that executed the order to uproot everybody in Holden Street was similarly Faustian: indirect and impersonal. Only now, in its modern incarnation, it is mediated not by devilish spirits but by complex professional organisations and institutional roles, which likewise wash their hands of the job, and disavow the jobber once the work is done.

Cantril Farm was a master plan designed and administered by architects, planners and bureaucrats who were just going about their professional business, doing so 'efficiently', following rules. But when I think about Cantril Farm and my Nan today, and when I think about Faustian professionals, there are a few twists to what we might take from this episode. For one thing, it's clear that a lot has changed in the world of professionalism – its ideals and practices have changed, down to the very nature of who the professionals are. Back then we dealt with *public* welfare professionals; or rather, public professionals dealt with us. Now, the professional world is dominated by commercial interests, by *private* professionals, business professionals – or at least by professionals who collapse any distinction between public and private. By the late 1970s, projects like Cantril Farm had turned into sink estates deeply affected by economic downturn in the wake of the global oil crisis of 1973. Fiscal crisis became the order of the day. Welfare statism came under fire, and soon public budgets were slashed, hitting cities like Liverpool, with its high rates of deindustrialisation and unemployment, especially hard. The 1980s bid adieu to a post-war era of social democratic reformism, undertaken by public professionals, an era when the public sector was seen as the solution to a decidedly bent private sector. But throughout the Thatcher and Reagan years, pundits and ideologues reversed the logic, presenting the private sector as the solution to a bloated and failing public sector. The promise of state professionals dishing out public goods under some vague ideal of equality gave way to an order in which the market was the panacea.

Since the 1980s, a new class of private professionals and experts has risen to prominence, no longer concerning themselves with redistributive social justice. Instead, they apply cost-benefit analysis to calculate efficiency models, devising new business paradigms for delivering social services at minimal cost. As a consequence, services have been contracted out to low-ball bidders and many government departments have been dissolved or replaced by new units of 'post-political' middle managers, answerable to technocrats and professional administrators whose machinations are as publicly transparent as mud.

In retrospect, the crises of the 1970s marked something of a turning point. They offered fresh opportunities for a different breed of professional. If anything, crises always seem to be an incubator for new professionals, 'expert' problem-solvers intervening in public affairs, supposedly above and beyond politics. As ever, the United States has been a trusty testing ground. In the 1970s, social welfare departments began shifting not only towards market solutions but also to approaches masterminded by independent think tanks. Think tanks and management consultants had been giving business advice to corporate America for decades; now they turned their attention to how governments should run government, how governments should downsize government, and how welfare should be reshaped.

One early think-tank solution to welfare policy was applied in fiscally strapped New York. In the 1970s, New York City's Mayor John Lindsay hired the RAND Corporation, a Santa Monica-based think tank, to assess how money could be saved from the city's fire department (FDNY). RAND computer analysts set about modelling city-wide fire patterns to help efficiently reorganise FDNY firehouses, reallocating public resources according to these patterns. This budget-trimming programme became part of a wider Federal policy known as 'Planned Shrinkage': the purposeful running-down of blighted neighbourhoods seen as no longer economically 'viable'. 'Shrinkage' was code for elimination, for the deliberate destruction of 'bad' communities across America – the problematic neighbourhoods that were a drain on public finances.

RAND had emerged in the late 1940s, growing out of the Douglas Aircraft Company, prospering initially from military contracts. A powerhouse of mandarin scientists and technocrats, including dozens of Nobel Laureates, RAND housed the mathematicians and physicists behind the US's nuclear defence strategy, Faustian men who devised the first atomic bomb and earliest modern computer. RAND's hallmark was 'systems analysis', a mode of thinking that could replace messy civic power politics with the cool rationality of numbers, calculated by some of the nation's smartest brains.

The fire-plagued South Bronx became a RAND laboratory. 'Game theory' models were built to replicate where, when and how often fires broke out in the Bronx. By measuring the lag between alarm call and the moment the fire truck arrived at the alarm box, RAND could predict how quickly – or slowly – FDNY fire trucks responded. By showing which areas received faster and slower responses, RAND determined which fire stations had less impact and thus were cost-ineffective. In other words, RAND highlighted which stations could be slashed from the public budget. And yet, as Joe Flood shows in his revealing book *The Fires*, response time was a lousy measure of firefighting operations.[3]

One of Flood's chapter titles pretty much says everything about RAND's 'scientific' shortcomings: 'Quantifying the Unquantifiable'. Response time had an appeal to number crunchers because it was easy to measure. But it falls well short of representing the realities of firefighting. In America's most congested city, RAND models never factored in how traffic played a role in response time. RAND also assumed that fire units were available to respond to alarm calls from the company station. But this is rare in the Bronx, where every truck is usually out over the entire borough, fighting fires at the same time.

RAND's sample size, meanwhile, was 'unrepresentative and poorly compiled', Flood says, and in the implementation of research RAND routinely dismissed crucial legwork as 'too laborious'; 'data discrepancies', they said, 'could be ignored for many planning purposes'. Finally, and most damning of all, RAND models 'fell prey to the very thing that technocracies are supposed to prevent: political manipulation. At the outset RAND studies didn't need to be manipulated – they provided what the politicians wanted.'

'Hoodlums didn't burn the Bronx', Flood concludes. The experts did. RAND's goal was to set a precedent that's now a norm throughout the world: to establish 'a new way of administering cities: use the mathematical brilliance of the computer modellers and systems analysts who had revolutionised military strategy to turn a corrupt, insular and unresponsive bureaucracy into a streamlined, non-partisan technocracy'. 'And so everyone was willing to look the other way as plans to close busy fire stations went into effect while the neighbourhood around burned to the ground'.

It's hard for bottom-up dissenters to contest top-down experts. The latter have a habit of dismissing the former as 'amateurs', as people *against* progress. We can see this at work again in New York, similarly in the 1970s, through that other assault on the public realm: 'Planned Shrinkage', the brainchild of Roger Starr (1918–2001). At different times in his life, Starr was New York City's housing commissioner, 'Urban Affairs' columnist at the *New York Times*, and executive director of New York Citizens' Housing and Planning Council, a real-estate-sponsored non-profit that still exists today. Yale-educated, Starr was a patrician elite intellectual, a former Trotskyist lefty who became a neoconservative righty. Throughout his career he worked hard to cast himself as a common-sense critic, as a no nonsense guy who cut through red tape.

In 1967, Starr published *Urban Choices: The City and Its Critics*, a series of influential essays that framed urban issues very much from the professional's standpoint.[4] The book is most revealing for the scorn heaped on 'well-intentioned amateurs', as Starr responds to 'the hundred critics' who dared to question professional urbanists – city officials, planners and architects, private developers, realtors, and of course Roger Starr himself. His roster of interferers reads like a Who's Who of popular, 'amateur' urbanists: Jane Jacobs, Saul Alinsky, Lewis Mumford, Ada Louise Huxtable, William H. Whyte, Herbert Gans.

To legitimise 'Planned Shrinkage', Starr launched tirades against the principle of 'community', suggesting it doesn't really exist in urban contexts, especially in urban America. Community is the flight of fancy of sentimental amateurs, who give it 'unearned veneration', he said. 'Critics', Starr thought, 'make a misleading assumption, an assumption in which they are cheerfully joined by a host of well-intentioned amateurs. They assume that the word community can safely be used to describe any human settlement in which more than two people live without assaulting each other. If one wants to keep the real world moving, however, community is a label to be used only when merited, like *Danger: Nitroglycerin*.'[5]

Since there's no such thing as community, it's all right to destroy neighbourhoods and forcibly move people on. 'American communities can be disassembled and reconstituted about as readily as freight trains', Starr believed. 'Stretches of empty blocks may be knocked down, services can be stopped and the land left fallow until a change in economic and demographic assumptions makes the land useful again'. Starr cites a report on Boston called *Grieving for a Lost Home*, which, he says, 'found that 26 per cent of women relocated were emotionally disturbed two years after the move'. 'Were they not "emotionally disturbed" before moving?' he wonders. Those who attack urban renewal, Starr says, 'have inferred that people living in areas to be renewed – where rents are low and physical deficiencies high – actually are well satisfied with their homes. With this assumption, I find myself in rather serious disagreement.'

Starr also found himself in serious disagreement with Jane Jacobs, the greatest of amateur urbanists and one who famously stood up to the developer Robert Moses (a man, like Starr, full of contempt for 'small' people). Starr can't quite address Jacobs on equal terms. Instead she's framed as a desperate housewife:

> Critics of the American city have been talking to it as a nagging wife addresses her drinking husband – in sublime confidence that the victim suffers from a simple disease, requiring only a simple remedy. If only, says the wife, you could stay away from that first highball when you leave the office ... If only, Jacobs tells the city [her husband], you didn't hang out with those nasty city planners, and left yourself alone ... You ought to take up a nice constructive hobby, like gardening, without artificial fertilisers.'[6]

In *Death and Life of Great American Cities*, Jacobs anticipates Starr and RAND's logic, and their 'intellectual' justification for an urban renewal based on numbers, pitted against low-income communities. It's only through statistical models, Jacobs wrote, that there 'arose the supposed feasibility of large-scale relocation of citizens. In the form of statistics, these citizens were no longer components of any unity except the family, and could be dealt with intellectually like grains of sand, or electrons or billiard balls. The larger the number of uprooted, the more easily they could be planned for on the basis of mathematical averages.'[7] 'What a dear, sweet character she isn't', said Starr of Jacobs. Jacobs called Starr 'a fool'. But Jacobs was onto how the professional techniques championed by the likes of Roger Starr and RAND were quack ideas, scientifically baseless, motivated by politics and vested interests.

In Britain, during the 1980s, the Tories nonetheless leapt on the bandwagon, and in some ways have never got off it, recycling 'Planned Shrinkage' in Liverpool after the 1981 Toxteth riots.[8] Thatcher's chancellor, Geoffrey Howe – now the late Lord Howe – thought Liverpool a lost cause. He drew up spending cuts under so-called Managed Decline, a forerunner of today's austerity orthodoxy.

Howe's plans only became public in 2011, under the thirty-year rule, which allows general access to National Archive files and Cabinet minutes. At the time, Howe was opposed to Environment Secretary Michael Heseltine's proposal for a regeneration fund to rebuild Liverpool's ruins and riot-hit communities, believing it a waste of government money. The problem of Liverpool, Howe felt, was 'the concentration of hopelessness', and its self-inflicted woes, what with industrial strife and citizens ransacking their own neighbourhoods. 'I cannot help feeling', said Howe, 'that the option of Managed Decline is one which we should not forget altogether. We must not expend all our limited resources trying to make water flow uphill.'[9]

In the late 1990s, Tony Blair and Gordon Brown's Labour Party began to steer its own course through 'non-partisan politics', returning to the source for inaugurating its 'target culture'. In a coda to his tale of Bronx fires, Joe Flood notes how New Labour 'developed an array of statistical tools to measure the job performance of everyone from sanitation workers to cabinet ministers. To cut costs and improve services, the British National Health Service was revamped along quantitative lines drawn up by Alain Enthoven, a onetime RAND analyst, a whiz-kid turned healthcare academic.'

꙰

I wonder sometimes whether the Cantril Farm saga might have been one subliminal reason why I got captivated by urban studies – the study of cities and the people who inhabit them, their social spaces and communities, their housing and infrastructure, their culture and politics. Going to college in the 1980s as a second-chance scholar, a twenty-something 'mature student', helped me better understand some of the literary loves I'd already developed in adolescence: Dostoevsky in St Petersburg, Baudelaire in Paris, Jack Kerouac in New York.

Hitherto my interest in cities had come through novels; now, doing Social Science at Liverpool Polytechnic, I was to study theory, urban theory, also sociology and geography, plus politics. It was an experience that changed my life, setting me on my way to the middle-aged person I've become today. At Liverpool Poly, I encountered dedicated, gifted humanities and social science teachers; most drank too much, hardly published anything, and were veritable antitheses of today's professionalised academy. They instilled in me a love for their subject. As teachers, they did something else, too: they let me into their lives, taught me how big ideas could resonate in life, not only on the page.

Later, I received a grant to go to Oxford University to study for a doctorate. I was fortunate enough to benefit from an era of free education, without which attending Oxford (and Liverpool Polytechnic for that matter) would have been impossible. But I wasn't bothered about Oxford itself, about going 'up' to such a place: all I wanted to do was work with the Marxist urbanist David Harvey, who'd just been installed as the Halford Mackinder professor of geography.

Harvey was – and still is – an outsider in the establishment, an amateur who shrugs off professionalism, who back then even shrugged off his Oxbridge title, hanging out with his graduate students rather than with his peers. Some of my most interesting conversations with him – my 'supervisions' – were carried out in Jericho's Bookbinders pub, playing bar billiards, or else at a local kids' playground around the corner, while he kept an eye on his young daughter. This highlighted for me two central pillars of intellectual amateurism: a *sensibility* to de-professionalise reality, and a political *allegiance* to ordinary folk. David just didn't act like a pro, and he still doesn't.

At Oxford in 1992, at the Sheldonian Theatre, I also had the privilege one evening to attend a lecture by Edward Said. The experience of seeing and hearing Said was very important for me; more important now than I'd recognised then, and pivotal for defining this book. At the time, he was a renowned professor of comparative literature at Columbia University, an Arab-American who spoke out against American foreign policy and its support for Israel, a tireless advocate of Palestinian rights. He came to blows not only with Zionists but also with Palestinian bigwigs. Said's views were independent, critical and controversial, honestly partisan, sceptical of any patriotic fervour (Palestinian included), and questioning of all corporate, class, racial and gender privilege.

The Sheldonian is Oxford University's ceremonial hall, designed by Christopher Wren and built in the 1660s. Said was there before a packed house, to present a dress rehearsal of his BBC Radio 4 Reith Lecture series, which would air shortly afterwards, on 'representations of the intellectual'. In it, Said distinguished the roles of amateur and professional intellectuals in knowledge production: one speaks truth *to* power, the other speaks the truth *of* power. Resplendent in Armani, expounding passionately on amateur intellectuals, on Joyce's Stephen Dedalus and Turgenev's Bazarov, on anti-heroes who refuse to serve authority, on thinkers who represent other values and prerogatives than profit and specialisation, Said struck an unforgettable figure.[10]

Said was calling out to intellectuals – and to budding intellectuals, as I was then – to reflect upon our craft and political engagement. Hearing him, I saw how I could frame what I already knew, and how I might channel future learning. He brought home that amateurism has nothing to do with whether you dress up or down. It goes beyond questions of competence, too, of being conscientious about what you do, and having the right skills to do it. Rather than solely an issue of practice, Said made me aware of the importance of making choices. He made me consider what was for sale, whether the goals I set myself were conformist or critical, and, perhaps most importantly, in whose interests I was acting.

'And yet', he continued, 'the question remains whether there is or can be anything like an independent, autonomously functioning intellectual, one who is not beholden to, and therefore constrained by, his or her affiliations with universities that pay salaries, political parties that demand loyalty to a party line, think tanks that while they offer freedom to do research perhaps more subtly compromise judgment and restrain the critical voice.'[11] In the nineteenth century, the intellectual was often an aloof type, a solitary non-conformist, a struggling poet or writer, an opium eater or hashish smoker, a bohemian off the radar of established opinion. In the twentieth century, intellectuals became more 'normalised'; the numbers of men and women belonging to a general group called intellectuals grew. They were journalists and professors, managers and computer experts, government officials and lobbyists, consultants and scientists, all of whom were usually remunerated for their knowledge wares.

The scope and diversity of intellectuals has expanded in our times. But this ushered in a problem, too, a split in what it means to be an intellectual. This is how Said framed the problem: 'The intellectual ought neither be so uncontroversial and safe as to be just a friendly technician, nor should they try to be a full-time Cassandra, who isn't only righteously unpleasant but also unheard.' Today, the situation has only become harder. Are there alternatives to 'total quiescence' or 'total rebelliousness'? Earlier generations had 'non-academic' intellectuals, like Jane Jacobs herself, who brought their critical and accessible scholarship to bear on popular social agendas; they *functioned* as intellectuals, even though they were never employed as such. A twenty-first-century intellectual is more likely to be an academic, with either no interest in dealing with the outside world or a little too much interest in dealing with the outside world, eagerly selling their opinions to the highest bidder.

It's the latter stance that Said sees as the greatest danger. 'The particular threat to the intellectual today', he said, 'isn't the academy, nor the suburbs, nor the appalling commercialism of journalism and publishing houses, but rather an attitude I will call *professionalism*'. Professionalism, he reckoned, 'means thinking of your work as an intellectual as something you do for a living, with one eye on the clock, and another cocked at what is considered to be proper, professional behaviour – not rocking the boat, not straying outside the accepted paradigms or limits, making yourself marketable and above all presentable.'

Professionalism as an attitude and job description comes with its own pressures. One is *specialisation*, an increasing technical formalism, a loss of sight 'of the raw effort of constructing either art or knowledge; as a result you can't view knowledge and art as choices and decisions, commitments and alignments, but only in terms of impersonal theories and methodologies.' Specialisation also kills your sense of excitement and discovery, your sense of curiosity. In fact, you no longer have curiosity, since specialisation means you're an 'expert' in such-and-such a field, and experts know everything, indeed *must* know everything, about it.

'Expert' becomes a pretext to say what you like within a certain context. It's an implicit denial of open-mindedness, of being inquisitive, of stretching your horizon. Experts affirm what they think they know matter-of-factly, never straying outside their specialist comfort zones, where they'd be unsure, like the rest of us. So it's in their professional interests to play safe; expert circles shrink, vistas narrow, intellectual curiosity diminishes. Experts can't drop their professional guard; an esoteric language sets them apart, gains entry into exclusive professional bodies, onto expert panels, ones strictly off-limits to rank amateurs, unless they're the audience.

Despite the pervasiveness of professionalism, Said thinks that it can be countered by courageous intellectual *amateurism*, an attitude that runs counter to professionalism. Anybody can do it, even professionals. It means a readiness to withstand comfortable and lucrative conformity, a desire, Said says, 'to be moved not by profit or reward but by love for and unquenchable interest in the larger picture, in making connections across lines and barriers, in refusing to be tied down to a specialty, in caring for ideas and values in spite of the restrictions of a profession'.[12]

This is a beautiful, inspiring rendering of what amateurism is all about. It's to uphold a vision of reality that's more expansive and eclectic, that isn't hampered by the conservatism of narrow expertise, preoccupied as that is with defending one's scholarly turf. To be an amateur is to express the ancient French word: *love of*, a person who engages for the pleasure of it. In many instances, amateurs are more competent than professionals, because they're more intimately connected to what they do. What they do is who they *are*.

Amateurs uphold ideas that oppose professional authority. They express concerns professionals don't consider, don't care about, often won't acknowledge. An amateur is more likely to be someone who rocks the boat. He or she isn't on anybody's payroll and never will be. To that degree, an intellectual ought to be an amateur, Said insists: a thinking and concerned member of society who raises questions at the very heart of professionalised activity. By doing so, you can reconnect to more meaningful, personal projects, to more original thoughts. It's a sense of self-worth, an affirmation of engaged activity that hinges on an audience and a constituency. Indeed, is that audience there to be satisfied, a client to be kept happy, Said wonders, or is it there to be challenged, provoked, stirred into opposition, mobilised into collective, democratic action?

2

A Question of Faith

The penetration of expert professionalism into everyday life runs deep, although sometimes it's hard to recognise. Oftentimes the rule of the expert isn't out in the open; it's not palpable, not fully present in such a way that we feel it. Instead, it lingers over us, impregnates us, filters through us. We live out its result, absorb its ideology, all of us, and it is difficult to resist. What happens is something akin to how the seventeenth-century theologian Blaise Pascal describes 'faith'. You *learn* to believe like an 'automaton', 'by habit'. Only faith here has little to do with any heavenly God. It's being faithful to an earthly belief system, society's dominant ideology of professionalism.

This ideology knows how to classify and quantify human reality, yet increasingly does so in the terms of religion rather than reason, as a theology rather than an epistemology. 'We must not misunderstand ourselves', Pascal says. 'We are as much automatic as intellectual; and hence it comes that the instrument by which conviction is attained is not demonstration alone. How few things can be demonstrated! Proofs only convince the mind. Habit is the source of our strongest and most believed proofs. It inclines the automaton, which persuades the mind without its thinking about the matter.'[1]

As we moved through the 1990s and into the 2000s, 'neoliberal' politicians pledged to shrink government and the public sector, to downsize both from our lives. They said that the public sector was inflated, inefficient and unwieldy. They promised to reduce bureaucracy, deregulate it, loosen its rigidity, slash its red tape. They brought in expert professional consultants to lead efficiency drives. In the US, the number of governmental committees to discuss 'Red Tape Reduction Acts' grew. From the 1960s to the 1990s, the tally of senior executives and political appointees in the federal bureaucracy quintupled. The average number of departmental levels between the president at the top and your ordinary bureaucrat at the bottom swelled from seventeen in the 1960s to thirty-two in the 1990s.

In Britain, there's been a similar thickening of government, despite claims of shrinkage. This reflects the aggrandisement of a professional political class, a growing stratum of ministers and special advisors, experts and researchers, complementing the expansion of non-governmental quangos and programmes that mix and match public and private, state and business. Since 2010, Tory politicians have vowed to reduce 'each and every quango', 'to cut the cost of bureaucracy and the number of public bodies', 'increase accountability', and impose 'efficiency, effectiveness and economy in the exercise of public funds'.[2]

More than five years on, 200 of these 766 non-departmental public organisations have gone. At the same time, other new bodies such as 'independent monitoring boards' have sprouted, and new 'executive agencies' in education, health, employment, and crime prevention have received the green light. Cost savings from Peter have duly gone to pay Paul, and in reality the process of government has grown less transparent while being equally, if not more, expensive. Much here, like in the US, has to do with targets and performance, those leaps of professional faith introduced by New Labour in the late 1990s. To monitor efficiency goals, an audit culture has meant more, not less, paperwork; new initiatives now keep a check on performance scores in all walks of social and administrative life.

This 'outcomes-based' approach focuses not only on results but also on their *measurability*. Millions are spent checking, auditing, defining and redefining, systematising and re-systematising targets and controls. Yet targets often fail in human terms, because the most important public services – health and education – aren't amenable to narrow measurement.[3] Successive governments have tried to measure what is largely unmeasurable, quantify what is unquantifiable, regulate what has already been deregulated. They've tried, in other words, to see things like a state.

Seeing Like a State is James C. Scott's treatise on why states often get it wrong. The text was published in 1998, a little while before our target culture was fully unleashed onto the world. But Scott lets us see with the eyes of the state in its early modern guise. Reading him, we realise how little has actually changed, because now, as then, the state regards things 'primarily through the fiscal lens of revenue needs'. It's a project, says Scott, sometimes heroic in its construction yet invariably blinkered: much falls outside its limited field of vision.

Scott, who studied South-East Asian peasants for years and was a great believer in local, vernacular wisdom, goes back to the development of scientific forestry in nineteenth-century Saxony. Lurking behind this science was a concern for cultivating wood commercially. Science became a handmaiden of 'official management'. Timber was relevant to shipbuilding, to state construction, to fuel, and was above all a matter of state revenue. The state had no interest in nature as such, only in 'natural resources', the parts of nature that could be appropriated for economic use, totted up according to all-too-human adjudication. The utilitarian state couldn't see the forest for the trees. Trees were products, taxes, revenue, profit, and yield. Moreover, within this narrow remit, highly prized animals were 'livestock' or 'game'; competing animals were 'predators' and 'pests', manufactured enemies.

'In state fiscal forestry', says Scott, 'the actual tree with its vast number of possible uses was replaced by an abstract tree representing a volume of lumber or firewood.'[4] Everything touching on intimate human interaction was erased. 'The state did pay attention to poaching, which impinged on its claim to revenue or its claim to royal game, but otherwise it typically ignored the vast, complex, and negotiated social uses of the forest for hunting and gathering, pasturage, fishing, foraging, charcoal making, trapping, and collecting food and valuable minerals as well as the forest's significance for magic, worship, and refuge'. State professionalism had no time for popular amateurism, for other systems of measurement and worth.

Scott grants certain achievements in German forestry science and in its standardising techniques. Decisive, though, was what this engendered for the next 'logical' step in forestry management. 'That step', he says, 'was to create, through careful seeding, planting, and cutting, a forest that was easier for state foresters to count, manipulate, measure, and assess.' 'The fact is that forest science and geometry, backed by state power, had the capacity to transform the real, diverse, and chaotic old-growth forest into a new, more uniform forest that closely resembled the administration grid of its techniques.'[5] It sounds a lot like what urban planners did to cities, and what healthcare and educational experts continue to do to hospitals, schools, and universities. In the end, says Scott, seeing like a state meant not seeing very much. Least of all a forest:

'the forest could be 'read' accurately from the tables and maps in the forester's office.'

Someone who once had the state look at him, as a delinquent American taxpayer, was the distinguished man of letters Edmund Wilson, author of the Marxist-Leninist classic *To The Finland Station* (1940). Throughout the late 1940s and 1950s, Wilson lived abroad and didn't file an income tax return. Surviving for years – like many writers acclaimed or otherwise – on a shoestring, piling up debts, he didn't think he was obliged to file anything, especially when there was so little income to pay tax on. But when he returned to the US, during the McCarthy era, as a suspected communist sympathiser, he was hit by a bullying bureaucracy. And, he discovered, it was a bullying bureaucracy equal to any bullying bureaucracy he'd witnessed in the Soviet Union.

'I had no idea at the time', Wilson says in his book *The Cold War and the Income Tax: A Protest* (1963), 'of how heavy our taxation had become or of the severity of the penalties exacted for not filing tax returns.' He quickly found out that the severity is greater for the little people; big organisations and rich citizens get away with it, having smart tax lawyers to represent them. The title of Wilson's text also said plenty about what was happening to US tax dollars: they were going up in a puff of smoke, fuelling the 'red threat', crowned by a colossally expensive chemical-bio-logical-radiological weapons programme.[6]

The other thing Wilson discovered was that one US Internal Revenue Service (IRS) department didn't know what other depart-ments were up to; disarray was patent, amid confusion and serial incompetence, exacerbated by Wilson's plight as a writer. It's the story of an amateur getting judged by professionals who had no sense of what amateurism entailed: 'Not even the best-trained lawyer can apparently find his way through the forest of those gigantic tax books, through the dense print and the obscurely worded sentences of those innumerable exasperating forms which involve supplying endless data about every detail of one's profit and losses, or of one's personal or corporate expenditures.'

The question of what should be taxed and what deducted 'has reached the point of fine-spun complexity', Wilson says, 'that – working in terms of a different set of values – recalls the far-fetched distinctions of medieval theology. You come to feel that there must be somewhere, in the midst of all this pedantry, busy minds that are amusing themselves with gratuitous paradoxes of reasoning.' 'I find it difficult', he continues,

> to think of anything I do or anywhere that I go which could not be called a business expense: the books I buy, the librar-ies I visit, my travel to foreign countries, a good deal of my entertaining, which keeps me in touch with the literary and learned world. What business has the government to demand of me that I itemise and justify all this? What right has the government to say which expenses are and which are not 'legitimate'? This is the realm of 'psychic value', with which no government can really deal.[7]

Bureaucracies can also wear you down through sheer profes-sional dullness. One of the greatest works written about the tedium of modern bureaucracy is *The Pale King*, by the late David Foster Wallace (1962–2008), a fictionalised and unfinished 'vocational memoir' about his time at the IRS in Peoria, Illinois, circa mid-1980s. Foster Wallace's novel features bureaucratic tax professionals 'who look at their watches out of reflex', have 'more scalp than hair', and display with pride 'Franklin Quest Time

Management certificates'. They have a 'classic look', he says, 'of unwilled tight confinement'. Bureaucracy, however, isn't 'a closed system', Foster Wallace emphasises. 'It is this that makes it a world instead of a thing.'

Foster Wallace enters into the living world of the most important federal bureaucracy in American life and shows how this living world deadens. He crops up as a character, too, a certain 'David Wallace', although after hundred pages or so David Wallace fades away into the system, 'becomes a creature of the system'.[8] Meanwhile Foster Wallace, the author, continues to sneak between the lines, intervening in his characters' thoughts, offering qualification and explication (including lengthy footnotes), with vignettes on the personal lives and inner psyches of IRS employees – those 'examiners' like Claude Sylvanshine, Ned Stecyk, Dick Tate and Lane Dean. A lot happens over 500 pages, notwithstanding Foster Wallace's main point that *nothing happens*: monotony prevails; stultifying boredom; the performance of mindless, pointless tasks. The challenge is how to pay attention, how to concentrate, despite what you're doing. How to keep human in a daily round reduced to such tedium?

'But here's the thing', Foster Wallace writes in a narrative that shifts between deep satire and sorrowful pity:

Both then and now, very few ordinary Americans know anything about all this. Nor much about the deep changes the Service underwent in the mid-1980s, changes that today directly affect the way citizens' tax obligations are determined and enforced. And the reason for this public ignorance is not secrecy. Despite the IRS's well-documented paranoia and aversion to publicity, secrecy here has nothing to do with it. The real reason why US citizens were not aware of these conflicts, changes, and stakes is that the whole subject of tax policy and administration is dull. Massively, spectacularly dull.[9]

'The memoir-relevant point here', Foster Wallace admits, 'is that I learned, in my time with the Service, something about dullness, information, and irrelevant complexity. About negotiating boredom as one would a terrain, its levels and forests and endless wastes.'[10] Here are some 'laws of IRS personnel':

All GS-9 Examiners want to be GS-11 Examiners. All GS-11 Examiners want to be Auditors. All Auditors want to be Appeals Officers or Supervisors. All Supervisors want to be Group Managers. All Group Managers want to be Deputy District Directors. All Deputy District Directors want to be District Directors. The best the District Director can do is make their District's output look really good and hope someone notices. Output is the ratio of collected tax to District expenses. It's the District's net profit.

Foster Wallace worked at the IRS midway through the Reagan years. Bureaucracy's birth-pangs then were the birth-pangs of *deregulation*. At that moment, we were on the cusp of witnessing how professional bureaucracies were themselves professionalising. Shifts in logic and mindset were evident. The foundational principles of what we have today were being formulated. 'Old IRS guard', Foster Wallace says, 'are driven by self-righteousness, tax cheats as deadbeats, tax payment as virtue.' Or else 'they're drab civil servants in it for security, standard government workers.' The new IRS guard, by contrast, are not only good accountants but good strategic and business planners: the whole point is to maximise revenue – disregard civic virtue, disregard the moral warrior aspect of being in tax collection. New Peoria REC Personnel guy is a new guard: his whole deal is finding employees and organising stuff so that examiners maximise the revenue that auditors can yield. His willingness to experiment/think in fresh ways leads, paradoxically, to deep mysticism: a certain set of numbers that lets examiners concentrate better. The ultimate point is the question whether humans or machines can do exams better, can maximise efficiency in spotting which returns might need auditing and will produce revenue.[11]

Foster Wallace's *The Pale King* lets us glimpse how the state sees and how bureaucracies see themselves. The IRS still sees us the way it saw Edmund Wilson. Its quest still is to maximise the revenue it can collect. Little apparently has changed there. Although it's true, too, that bureaucracy isn't quite what it was. Caricatures of bureaucracy hail from the 1950s, evoking the shabby, sad realm of pen-pushing alienation, of cubicles and plastic inboxes, of out-trays and ticks and crosses, of organisation men in grey flannel suits. Yet in many ways, it's no longer like that. Bureaucracy was once a place, an institution, a thing. Now, it's something else, something more; a world that has become a life-world, a life-world that's inside us.

Its professional organisation men are different, as well: slicker, more imaginative, more deviously powerful. They have different aspirations and set different targets, different standards. They're no longer pen-pushers but keyboard tappers. They've dispensed with the grey flannel suits and are smarter, more fashionable, or else wear T-shirts and jeans. Now, the infrastructure of bureaucracy has been transformed. What we have is a bureaucratic culture that anthropologist David Graeber calls a 'utopia of rules'. 'As the language of anti-bureaucratic individualism has been adopted', Graeber says, 'with increasing ferocity', attempts 'to make government more "efficient" have been made through partial privatisation of services and the incorporation of ever-more "market principles", "market incentives", and market-based "accountancy processes" into the structure of the bureaucracy itself.'[12] Thus, every initiative 'to reduce red tape and promote market forces will have the ultimate effect of increasing the number of regulations'.

Rules and regulations are everywhere and seemingly nowhere. We're told they don't exist, that we are freer, live with less red tape. Like all good utopias, bureaucracy is a non-place, a figment of our own febrile collective imagination. But it's equally an all-too-terrible concrete reality. Bureaucracy, we might say, is in denial. It has been 'suspended from its immediate form'. This language here is Karl Marx's, from the *Grundrisse*, where he wrote about labour and fixed capital. Marx calls fixed capital the physical infrastructure – factories, machinery, warehouses, docks, offices, roads – that enables capital to circulate and accumulate. Bureaucracy has shed its material fetters; it is no longer subsumed under the sway of the fixed capital of an institution, of an office building or other localised physical entity: it has been absorbed as a system within everyday life, subsumed under the principles of efficiency, dictated by faith in science and technology. These days, everyday life is a professional bureaucratic system. To live it out is to enter into a system, into the technological application of science; it imbues everything, everywhere we go.

We ourselves are a sort of living fixed capital, organic commercial and administrative infrastructure. Bureaucracy has *deterritorialised* from its static, fixed casing, and *reterritorialised* inside us. We are its walking hardware and software, its portable filing system. Nowhere is this more palpable than in *self-bureau-cratisation*. New technology and social media have increased our individual liberty and helped foster self-responsibility, enabling us to handle our affairs ourselves. But its paperless bureaucracy is now all-encompassing. From smartphone banking to online filing of tax returns, from paperless paying of utility bills to PayPal and Amazon accounts, from emailed Apple receipts to internet and phone contracts, from car insurance to travel bookings, you name it. Each with an infinite array of personal passwords and pass-codes, complex numbering and lettering, symbolic ordering and secure encoding – all needing to be memorised.

We're increasingly in the thrall of a 'virtual' bureaucracy, a total administration with neither forms nor administrators, without apparent bureaucrats, a bureaucracy internalised in us, a self-bureaucracy. It's as if life has slid somewhere between Franz Kafka's two great novels, *The Trial* (1925) and *The Castle* (1926), marking an epochal shift in our administered (and self-administered) pro-fessionalised world. In *The Trial*, Josef K., 'like a dog', stands accused before an omnipotent tribunal, a sort of state-monopoly capitalist system of old, where bureaucracies were public institu-tions that directly intruded upon us. They sent us letters, moved us on, disciplined us, dictated the rules, came to arrest us. 'You can't leave because you're under arrest', the police tell Josef K. at the beginning of *The Trial*. 'And why am I under arrest?' K. asks. 'That's something we're not allowed to tell you.'[13]

In *The Castle*, there's no longer anyone to arrest you; you arrest yourself. Now the protagonist K. inhabits a world that's suddenly shrunken into a village, whose castle on the hill seems more dom-inant and elusive than ever before. K. can't find a policeman even when he needs one. In this village with its castle, we can glimpse our own 'global village', our world compressed by globalisation and technology. The psychological drama of one man confronting a castle is a political parable of all of us today – having to conceive a collective identity to resolve a gothic bureaucratic mystery. 'Are there control authorities?' K. wonders of the castle. 'There are nothing but controlling authorities', the mayor tells him. After a while, K. begins to catch on: 'Nowhere', he sighs, 'had he seen officialdom and life as interwoven as they were here, so interwoven that it sometimes looked as if officialdom and life had changed places.'[14]

Officialdom and life was something Kafka knew about first-hand. He was a professional bureaucrat himself. In the early decades of the twentieth century, he rose to deputy head of his department at the Workers' Accident Insurance Institute in Prague, officiating on workingmen's compensation. Kafka used his combination of technical, insurance, and legal knowledge to dismiss protests from business bosses. They grumbled that their working conditions were far less dangerous than Institute actuaries supposed. Kafka deployed his writing skills to great effect, too, drafting reports and convincing courts. By all accounts, he was a formidable opponent for corporate lawyers; eloquent and mild-mannered, he knew his subject inside out.[15]

Kafka may have saved thousands of workers' lives and been one of the early brains behind occupational health and safety legislation. Rather than a cog in an unfathomable machine, he seems to have been a creative bureaucrat. So what was his problem? What was Kafka telling us in his novels? Was he, an insider who knew, warning of the increasingly expansive powers of a bureaucratic system taking hold in the world?

Kafka's working life became very much entwined with his literary life, even though he said they were 'mutually exclusive'; 'writing', he wrote, 'has its centre of gravity in depth, whereas the office is on the surface of life.' As far as literature went, Kafka was a rank amateur: he wrote in his spare time – late at night – and made no money from it; indeed, he was barely published in his lifetime. By 1912, as his output grew, he saw the Workers' Insurance Institute as the enemy of his creative imagination. That was maybe what he took against. It was crushing his ability to express himself.

Perhaps the most inspiring and tragic of Kafka's insights comes in the penultimate paragraph of *The Trial*: 'Logic is doubtless unshakable, but it cannot withstand a person who wants to go on living.' Tragic, because Kafka has Josef K. say it too late; he's already done for. He proves Kafka wrong. Or maybe K. has given up wanting to live? Kafka seems to be sending us a warning: he doesn't want us to reach this fatal point, to go over the edge ourselves. He doesn't want us to accept our guilt at the behest of some bureaucratic ideology. We know K. is done for when, at the cathedral, the prison chaplain calls out to him. 'His cry was unambiguous and there was no escape from it: Josef K.!'

K. had his chance to ignore this cry, to keep walking, 'to simply appear that he had not understood or that he had understood but chose not to pay attention'. Yet instead he turned around, 'he acknowledged that he had understood perfectly well, that he really was the Josef K. the priest had called.'[16] It was only then that the priest could utter the *coup de grâce*: 'You don't need to accept everything as true, you only have to accept it as necessary.' 'How depressing', responds K. 'It makes world order dependent on this lie.'

In *The Castle*, K. encounters a somewhat different conundrum. Bureaucratic authority seems to have undergone a strange kind of deregulation. Whereas in *The Trial* the authorities and courts were distant, even unknowable (occupying unlikely attic rooms in poor tenement blocks), in *The Castle*, 'dealing directly with the authorities was not particularly difficult.' 'Rather', Kafka writes,

> they let K. go anywhere he liked – of course only within the village – and thus pampered and enervated him, ruled out all possibility of conflict, and transported him into an unofficial, totally unrecognised, troubled, and alien existence. So it came about that while a light and frivolous bearing, a certain deliberate carelessness was sufficient when one came in direct contact with the authorities, one needed in everything else the greatest caution, and had to look round on every side before one made a single step.[17]

Kafka here seems to be onto our 'post-political' conjuncture. Nowadays, the ubiquitous castles that reign over us are frequently in plain view, visible and palpable to our senses; yet at the same time, they're distant and somehow cut off, out of reach, inaccessible. Kafka is better than Marx at recognising the thoroughly modern organisational mystery besieging people today. Marx understood the dynamics of the production of castles and the economic ordeals this system subjects us to. But he was less sensitive to its corridors of power, and how its organisational bureaucracies functioned.

Marx grasped the difficulty of struggling against an economic process of producing capital. Kafka, however, intuited that this process would one day necessitate vast administrative management, beyond the massively complex divisions of labour: it would also involve even more massive bureaucratic compartmentalisations, ordained by unaccountable, anonymous technocrats and bureaucrats. Kafka imagined how modern conflict is an us-against-a-world transformed into an immense, and invariably abstract, total administration.

Such a vast administration sucks everything into a singular and unified spiralling force, into a seamless organisational web that has effectively collapsed and amalgamated different layers and boundaries. Erstwhile distinctions between the political and the economic, between conflict and consent, between politics and technocracy, between administration and self-administration, have lost their specific gravity and their clarity of meaning: integration functions through a conflating process of co-optation and corruption, of re-appropriation and re-absorption, of blocking off by breaking down. Each realm now simply elides into its other, and it's up to ordinary people to find a way out.

Where K. goes astray in *The Castle*, and where his quest borders on the hopeless, is in his struggle to access the castle's occupants; he wants to penetrate the stronghold's bureaucratic formalities and the 'flawlessness' of its inner circle. K. struggles for a way in rather than a way out. Using all the Cartesian tools of a land surveyor, he confronts the castle on the castle's own terms, on its own ostensibly 'rational' frame of reference. He wants to render the world of the castle intelligible, as opposed to rendering it unacceptable. He makes rational complaints when rationality has turned into superstition, into an act of pure professional faith.

Of course, K.'s task would have been less *Kafkaesque* if this professional total administration were based on rationality. But we know it isn't, whatever the classic literature on bureaucracy may claim. At the turn of the twentieth century, the German sociologist Max Weber saw rationality much as we might commonly see it today: as a method associated with science, a perception founded on reason rather than faith, a rigorous objectivity. To be rational is thus to operate on the basis of analysable, general rules and statutes. Rationality, for Weber, is akin to good 'book-keeping':

empirically oriented, quantifiable, open to precise calculation and systematic measurement.

Weber regarded bureaucracies as rational because they function though organising, reorganising, and streamlining principles. They create out of an ever-more complex and advanced reality an ever-more complex and advanced form of managing this reality. For Weber, an elaborate, efficient, and rationally organised reality is favourable to the greater good of society. Compared to previous civilisations, he said, modern industrial capitalism bases itself on science and technology, and, in so doing, enlarges the extent to which rationality can be practiced – or seems able to be practiced. In antiquity,

> bureaucracy stifled private enterprise. There is nothing unusual in this, nothing peculiar to Antiquity. Every bureaucracy tends to intervene in economic matters with the same result. Whereas in Antiquity the policies of the city-state necessarily set the pace for capitalism, today capitalism itself sets the pace for bureaucratisation of the economy. Thus in all probability someday the bureaucratisation of society will encompass capitalism too, and we will then all enjoy the benefits of bureaucratic 'order'.[18]

Weber's contemporary, Sigmund Freud, saw rationality in a quite different light. Rationality, for Freud, is basically a process where you invent a justification for your actions; a person might actually believe in these justifications, even though their belief is groundless. Rationality is about self-convincing, about a self-retelling of the same story over and over, until it becomes self-evidently true – rational. From this standpoint, 'rational actions' are manifestations of personality disorders, and serve entirely different, largely unconscious goals. Entering into the 'rational' mind of a professional bureaucracy is thus to enter into the mind of a collective obsessive-compulsive disorder. Organisational ideals are tantamount to expert fantasies, idealised wish-images of people with ego-centred desires. Collective ideals here both reflect and deflect individual ego-ideals. The clash is what Freud took to be the root of 'civilisation and its discontents'.

Half a century before Weber and Freud, a young Karl Marx was touching on both their visions in his *Critique of Hegel's Philosophy of Right*. In 1843, Marx suggested that there's a 'buffer' created by bureaucracies between the 'Corporation' (commerce) and the state (government). Any bureaucracy, for it to survive, must defend 'the imaginary universality of particular interests'.[19] In organisations, particular administrations exist in which 'personal arbitrariness is broken against authorised bodies'. This imaginary universality is important, because it acts as a collective ideological ballast against particular interests. But these particular interests gnaw away at the imaginary universal, tend to undermine it in their own self-interests. As such, 'the individual Corporation has the will for its own particular interest in opposition to the bureaucracy'.

This dialectic between the universal and the particular must be transcended. The whole must prevail over the sum of its parts: 'The bureaucracy as the completed Corporation must win the day over the Corporation which acts like an incomplete bureaucracy.' An inexorable battle ensues, which is still ongoing: 'The Corporation is civil society's attempt to become a state; but the bureaucracy is the state which has really made itself into civil society.' Thus a sort of rationality prevails, staving off both particular flights of fancy and collective autocracy. At least that's the theory.

In practice, it's a no-exit, a prisoner's dilemma, and, sounding a lot like Kafka, Marx reckons 'the bureaucracy is a circle from which no one can escape'. 'The highest point entrusts the under-standing of particulars to the lower echelons, whereas these, on the other hand, credit the highest with an understanding in regard to the universal; thus they deceive one another.' 'The general spirit of the bureaucracy is secret, the mystery, preserved inwardly by means of hierarchy and externally as a closed Corporation.' What emerges is a weird collective state of mind, a paranoid state, per-taining to faith rather than reason – 'the *bureaucratic mind*', Marx calls it. 'The bureaucratic mind', he says, 'is through and through a Jesuitical, theological mind ... The bureaucracy is a tissue of practical illusion.' 'Bureaucrats', Marx concludes, 'are the Jesuits and theologians of the state.'

Here we seem to have come full circle, back to Pascal and the realm of 'practical illusion'; to a form of professional organisa-tion based on the 'universal illusion', on numbers and targets, on a belief rather than a truth. We're also back to thinking about how these illusions might be confronted, even punctured. Almost all the literature challenging bureaucratic totalitarianism por-trays two scenarios of oppositional dissent: one, broadly that of Kafka's K., pits a rational anti-hero against a bizarrely irrational machine, elusive and surreal in its machinations. The other, which is Dostoevsky's Underground Man, pits a terrifyingly rational machine against a bizarrely surreal anti-hero.

The revolt of Dostoevsky's Underground Man is perhaps the more suggestive, because it's less 'rational' and potentially more subversive. His problem, though, is that he obsesses so rabidly about the rationality of official authority that he's blind to its irra-tionality. The Underground Man doesn't launch a rational tirade against authoritarian society: his critique is an expression of an individual's capricious, irrational desire. If professional systems internalise algorithmic logic, he is its poetic, humanistic nemesis, an amateur deviant, a living anti-system.

He could never accept the numbing routine of the 'bureaucratic mind', of a life dictated by mathematical formulas and algorithms, even if he admits that sometimes 'two times two equals four is a fine thing'. Yet after two times two equals four, he thinks, 'there's nothing left to do, or even to learn'. Everything thereafter will be computed and designed with exactitude. There will be no more actions or adventures. 'Well, I wouldn't be surprised in the slightest if, suddenly, for no particular reason, in the midst of the universal future rational well-being, somebody … were to appear and, putting their hands on their hips, would say to us all: "How about it, why don't we knock this rational well-being into smithereens with one swift kick, with the sole purpose of sending all these logarithms to the devil!"'[20]

The Underground Man sees a society of logarithms and mathematical laws as symbolised by the Crystal Palace, Joseph Paxton's famous centrepiece to London's 1851 Great Exhibition. He gasps for breath at Paxton's masterwork, the incarnation of ultimate truth, but recoils at the thought of living in a society modelled on it: 'You feel that here something has been achieved, that here there is victory and triumph. No matter how independent you might be, for some reason you become terrified. "Hasn't the ideal in fact been achieved here?" you think. "Isn't this the ultimate? Isn't it in fact necessary to accept this as the truth fulfilled and grow dumb once and for all?"'

The Crystal Palace had already captured the imagination of Russian reformers, and the Underground Man was responding to them. Paxton's building had inspired Nikolay Chernyshevsky's radical utopia, descriptions of which form the most radiant passages of his novel *What Is to Be Done?* which appeared in 1863, two years before Dostoevsky's *Notes from Underground*. One of the key scenes in Chernyshevsky's book has protagonist Vera Pavlovna dream of human perfectibility,

> a building, an enormous building, such as are now in but a few capitals … or no, there is not a single one like that now! … no, but there is one that points towards it – the palace which stands on Sydenham Hill. Glass and steel, steel and glass, and that is all. No, that is not all, that is only the shell of the building … But there, inside, there is a real house, an enormous house. It is covered by this crystal and steel building as by a sheath … Life is healthy and quiet here. It preserves freshness.[21]

It may preserve freshness, but the Underground Man wants to fight shy of such an edifice. He vows to stick his tongue out at it, and at any society formulated on its logic. He's no 'piano key', he says, no 'organ stop'; no computer keyboard. His utopia can never be computated. His biggest fear is that the Crystal Palace presages a new phase of human life: 'New economic relations will commence, ready-made and likewise calculated with mathematical precision, so that all possible questions will vanish instantaneously, simply because all possible answers will have been provided for them.'

And yet, it's a funny thing rereading Dostoevsky's *Notes from Underground* today, thinking that professionalised bureaucracy – our latter-day Crystal Palace – is based on rationality. It certainly claims to calculate with mathematical precision. It certainly purports to follow the logic of two times two equals four. But the problem with two times two equals four is that most professionals accept its principle, yet end up sticking their tongues out at it, too. When it suits, they behave just as irrationally as the

Underground Man; they try to affect their collective desires, their political impulses. In their bureaucratic minds, sometimes 'two times two equals five is a very fine thing'. Their numbers might be straight but they can be bent to suit targets, calibrated according to belief systems and theological professional predicates.

3

The Measure of Knowledge

When I was an undergraduate, I remember one of my Polytechnic lecturers, Trevor Jones, being greatly amused by a scene from Marx's *Capital*. Cough-balls of smoker's laughter erupted, punctuated by rattlings of phlegm, as he recited aloud Marx lampooning a certain Nassau W. Senior: 'One fine morning, in the year 1836, Nassau W. Senior, a man famed both for his economic science and his beautiful style, was summoned from Oxford to Manchester, to learn in the latter place the political economy he taught in the former. The manufacturers chose him as their prize-fighter.'[1] I can hear another leap of laughter from Jones's throat as I write these lines now.

Nassau W. Senior was an eminent professor at Oxford University, an 'economic *bel esprit*', Marx called him. He seems to embody everything Marx loathed about English political economy, loathed about *academic* political economy: class bias masquerading as rigorous scholarship. Marx never used the term 'professional knowledge', but that's what he was identifying: knowledge produced by a professional representative, channelled through the authority of a rich, powerful, internationally renowned institution. And this wasn't simply professional knowledge: it was knowledge that bore the stamp of 'science', 'economic science'.

Marx, conversely, was a complete outsider, a trained philosopher but an autodidact in economic affairs. Unaffiliated and frequently destitute, he sat alone in the Reading Room of London's British Museum scribbling away at his magnum opus, *Capital: A Critique of Political Economy*. He had no professional badge of credibility to invoke. His was no economic science in the professional sense of the term. He was an avowed socialist, adept at critiquing ruling-class knowledge, a foreigner, easily dismissible by the professional powers-that-be. He was, above all else, an *amateur*.

But as an amateur, Marx took to task Senior's infamous 'Last Hour'. With Senior, Marx argued, Oxford credentials are mobilised to legitimise flimsy scholarship. With Senior, we witness the time-served ties existing between the academy and industry, with the former acting as the 'intellectual' mouthpiece of the latter. Senior had been summoned to Manchester, the seat of the international textile trade, to do battle for the manufacturers. He was their chosen 'prize-fighter'; his economic science was ammunition to defeat struggles to reduce the factory working day.

Marx highlights how Senior went to great technical lengths, invoking much numerical data, to argue that if the working day was reduced from twelve to ten hours all the manufacturers' profit would be destroyed. It would also destroy the workers' livelihoods, because along with profits, money for wages would go, too. Everybody would lose out. In the eleventh hour, Senior said, the worker reproduced their wages, and in the twelfth – the so-called 'Last Hour' – the manufacturers' profit. To cut the working day to ten hours would thus eliminate both. As Marx says, 'and the Professor calls this "analysis!"'

These are 'extraordinary notions', Marx writes, and he spends several pages meticulously denouncing ideology dressed up as 'analysis'. Senior grovels before the manufacturers, Marx says:

'The heart of a man is a wonderful thing, especially when it is carried in his wallet.' At one point, Senior tries to lend scientific credence to child labour exploitation. He suggests there's a 'warm and moral atmosphere in the factory', which keeps children out of mischief and safe from vice, beyond the grasp of their idle parents. Elsewhere, Marx questions the accuracy of Senior's figures. Finally, 'apart from errors in its content, Senior's presentation is confused'.

Marx explains that the source of profit emerges from 'surplus labour time', the time a worker spends beyond the 'necessary labour time' of earning their wages and recuperating manufacturers' overheads. The longer the working day, and the lower the wages, the greater the surplus labour amassed. Surplus labour time is the source of 'surplus value', and surplus value is, in turn, the real source of profit. None of which has anything to do with any 'Last Hour' of work. 'This faithful "last hour", about which you have invented more stories than the millenarians about the Day of Judgment, is', Marx concludes, 'all bosh'. I can hear in my head yet another peal of laughter from Jones.

But the bosh of Senior's 'Last Hour' nonetheless has its latter-day reincarnation. In the 1830s, an Oxford professor was the manufacturers' prize-fighter; 170 years on, the financiers of our day have found theirs – in two Harvard professors. In early 2010, Carmen Reinhart and former IMF chief economist Kenneth Rogoff published 'Growth in a Time of Debt' in the *American Economic Review*, a distinguished professional economic journal. The pair argued that nations with a public debt burden of more than 90 per cent of Gross Domestic Product (GDP) have in the past experienced stunted growth and economic stagnation; chances are, this trend will continue. As such, public debt must be purged. When a crisis hits and hurts, rather than use state monies to support needy people and battered economies, Reinhart and Rogoff invoke data to authorise its very antithesis: public-sector downscaling. The 90-per-cent rule is the Last Hour of austerity wisdom.

At the time, countries around the world were trying to deal with the fallout of the 2008 financial crisis, triggered by the US's 'subprime' housing market. This ushered in a period of perilous global economic instability. For a while, it seemed that capitalism itself teetered on the edge of implosion. Complete collapse was staved off only by state intervention, as governments supplied 'too-big-to-fail' banks with the necessary liquidity and capital to keep them afloat. The public expenditure required to bail neo-liberal capitalism out created fiscal deficits and a widespread crisis of public debt, affecting not only hard-hit countries like Greece and Spain, but also the cohesion of the European Monetary Union.

The debate that took hold on both sides of the Atlantic was whether Keynesian expansionary policies, involving high levels of borrowing to finance more government spending, should continue or be wound down. Reinhart and Rogoff's prescription sealed the issue: borrowing to finance public spending should cease; governments must balance their budgets and stabilise debt. As *New York Times* columnist Paul Krugman observed, 'Reinhart and Rogoff may have had more immediate influence on public debate than any previous paper in the history of economics.'

Within weeks of publication, George Osborne, then heir-apparent to the chancellor's office, addressed Conservative austerity faithfuls, citing 'Growth in a Time of Debt' as gospel. 'So', said Osborne, 'while private sector debt was the cause of this crisis, public sector debt is likely to be the cause of the next one.' This was the subtle non-sequitur that moved from induction to conjecture: the onus was shifted from the private sector to the public sector, without a shred of evidence. Osborne continued:

As Ken Rogoff himself puts it, 'there's no question that our most significant vulnerability as we emerge from recession is the soaring government debt. It's very likely that that will trigger the next crisis as governments have been stretched so wide.' ... To entrench economic stability for the long term, we need fundamental reform of our fiscal policy framework ... As I have made clear, our aim will be to eliminate the bulk of the structural current budget deficit.

Few people in the professional world objected to Osborne's speech, least of all Reinhart and Rogoff. Austerity-minded politicians in the US and Europe, like Paul Ryan, former chairman of the US House Budget Committee, and Olli Rehn, a top economist at the European Commission, nodded with approval. Meanwhile, 'Growth in a Time of Debt' was grist in the drafting of the Bowles-Simpson report for the National Commission on Fiscal Responsibility and Reform, created by the Obama administration in 2010. Yet in subsequent months, Reinhart and Rogoff's data were picked apart, first by a conscientious graduate student at a less prestigious college, University of Massachusetts Amherst, and then by his teachers, all of whom showed how the entire argument of Reinhart and Rogoff's article, and austerity's whole received wisdom, was effectively groundless.

For his graduate class, twenty-five-year-old PhD student Thomas Herndon was given an assignment: choose any economics paper and try to replicate its results. Herndon looked at 'Growth in a Time of Debt'. Try as he might, he couldn't replicate Reinhart and Rogoff's results. At first Herndon didn't believe it. He thought he'd erred somewhere. But he checked and rechecked, and rechecked his rechecking. Nothing doing; he still failed to reproduce the Harvard economists' findings. Herndon realised it was down to basic coding errors, major omissions (Australia, Austria, Belgium and Canada weren't in the historical analysis), and questionable weightings (for example, one year of negative growth in New Zealand in 1951 matched with twenty years' positive growth in the UK).

He took these discoveries to his Amherst professors and together they wrote a response. 'We find', they said, 'that coding errors, selective exclusion of available data, and unconventional weighting of summary statistics lead to serious errors that inaccurately represent the relationship between public debt and GDP growth among 20 advanced economies in the post-war period.' The Amherst team found that when properly calculated, the average real GDP growth rate for countries carrying a public-debt-to-GDP ratio of over 90 per cent is actually 2.2 per cent, not - 0.1 per cent. Contrary to what Reinhart and Rogoff conclude, average GDP growth at public debt/GDP ratios over 90 per cent isn't dramatically different than when debt/GDP ratios are lower.[2] Thus, there's no evidence that public debt burdens greater than 90 per cent of GDP reduce growth and no reason to cut public sector budgets. But facts are secondary when conclusions can be mobilised by powerful people to justify their own ends, through their own means.

In our professionalised times, it's clear that numbers are no laughing matter: they *count*. They seem to constitute believable, authoritative knowledge, an absolute knowledge that can be measured and managed. Numbers condition policy, and politicians like the numbers that best suit their political ambitions and career needs. They seek out experts who can provide them with the 'right' numbers. Many such experts come from academia, often from Ivy League economics departments. Numbers underwrite the algorithms that are the most powerful arbiters of our lives. They condition public service provision and educational opportunities, the news we read and the jobs we get, the ads we see and the information we apparently need to know.

We're living through a knowledge revolution, an era in which massive data sets purportedly reflect objective truth. 'Big Data' is the tag widely used to emphasise the sheer scale and abundance of information existing today, data picked up from our credit cards and mobile phone calls, from text messaging and social media images, from GPS signals and face recognition software. Smartphones come equipped with health apps and monitors that collect data from our daily routine; other wearable tech gadgets – like Microsoft's digital Alice band – keep tabs on everything we do.

Every aspect of our everyday life is cached and measured, counted and quantified. Then it's given a price. Behind this harvesting of data are grandiose claims that its predictive capabilities ensure better governance and a more efficient life, more vibrant cities and happier people, greater knowledge and increased wealth. Lucrative opportunities abound, especially for experts and for large corporations like Google, IBM, Cisco Systems and Siemens, who push through their latest product packages, offering all-encompassing fixes that governments pounce on. Political and civic life gets handed over to big business in exchange for the promise of optimisation.

What's significant here is the idea that these data are value neutral, without prejudice, beyond ideology. But algorithms tell us only what some people decide we need to know. The rationale behind which data need collecting – or not collecting – is frequently obscured from view. Likewise it's not clear how we should interpret and assess the implications of these data. Numbers are representations of reality, not reality itself, and behind each representation lie expert representatives.

The most succinct definition of Big Data is by Oxford University internet gurus Viktor Mayer-Schönberger and Kenneth Cukier: 'n = all'. Now we're no longer talking about a sample, because here Big Data supposedly includes everyone and everything. Thus n = all, where n equates to the entire population, handily doing away with any sampling bias; there's no longer any such thing as 'raw' data.[3] Other Big Data cheerleaders proclaim 'The End of Theory': experts can now accumulate enough data that the numbers speak for themselves. No more conjecture, no more speculation, no more deduction, no more conceptualisation – only the induction of numbers in 'theory-free' analysis.

Even scientific method is considered obsolete. 'This is a world', *Wired Magazine* wrote several years back, 'where massive amounts of data and applied mathematics replace every other tool that might be brought to bear. Out with every theory of human behaviour, from linguistics to sociology. Forget taxonomy, ontology, and psychology. Who knows why people do what they do? The point is they do it, and we can track and measure it with unprecedented fidelity.' Meanwhile, 'we can throw the numbers into the biggest computing clusters the world has ever seen and let statistical algorithms find patterns where science cannot.'[4]

Yet despite the promise and hyperbole, is it really possible to collect enough data for a perfect prediction, one that covers all the bases and helps inform democratic decision-making? Data sets are, after all, creations of fallible human minds. And some minds are more fallible than others. Humans give numbers their voice. We draw inferences from numbers, define their meaning, make interpretations, put them to use in ways we think appropriate. We include some things, and conveniently leave others out. We apply weightings and codings. We can certainly collect lots of data, but surely not *all* data; we can only ever work from incomplete data sets. Our algorithms can only ever make predictions on the basis of calculated averages.

In other words, Big Data might be big but it's still only a partial reflection of our complex reality; and even this partial reflection appears to us through a misted mirror. Isn't there something missing from a total algorithmic approach to our lives and destinies? Isn't there a difference between Google translating a language it doesn't know and speaking that language fluently yourself? Is a society really knowledgeable when it matches ads to content without any knowledge about either ad or content?

One issue here is that, willy-nilly, we implicate ourselves in these data sets. We are all children of a Petabyte Age. Kilobytes were put on our old floppy disks; megabytes on hard drives; terabytes on assorted USB keys. Now, petabytes, equivalent to about 20 million four-door filing cabinets, containing 500 billion pages, get stored on the Cloud. Everywhere we go, we develop tremendous data streams that allow others to predict what we'll do next. We harvest our own data: an estimated 60 per cent of people between sixteen and thirty-four years old use self-quantifying devices – from sleep monitors and pedometers, to geolocators and apps telling us where we can park our cars. All these data can be collated and owned by large corporations whose software is converted into big profits.

Thus the thing about Big Data: its *size*, such that only rich institutions can amass and process it, disseminate and monopolise it. Only big business can count up those big numbers. All sorts of metrics and algorithms emerge from Big Data, some true, many false. Glitches are invariably brushed off, cast aside using abstruse expert euphemisms like 'signal error' or 'confirmation bias'. But the truth is that Big Data is only as big or as small as the mind analysing it, as reliable or manipulable as the prize-fighters who champion it.

Every university, too, seems to be collecting and analysing Big Data, selling and encouraging research around Big Data, using it to forecast diverse aspects of humanity, from climate change to Walmart's sales performance. Here's the *Harvard Business Review* take, apropos Big Data, making it clear who's working for whom:

> The MIT Media Lab used location data from mobile phones to infer how many people were in Macy's parking lots on Black Friday – the start of the Christmas shopping season in the US. This made it possible to estimate the retailer's sales on that critical day even before Macy's itself had recorded those sales. Rapid insights like these can provide an obvious competitive advantage to Wall Street analysts and Main Street managers.[5]

The global management consultancy firm McKinsey is also muscling in on the act, working in partnership with MIT's Center for Digital Business and the Wharton Business School, helping US companies perform better, embracing 'Big Data-decision-making'. The group tested out a hypothesis that data-driven companies would be better performers. They conducted structured interviews with executives at 330 public North American companies about their organisational and technology management practices, gathering performance data from annual reports and independent sources. Companies in the top third of their industry using data-driven decision making were, MIT research illustrated, on average 5 per cent more productive and 6 per cent more profitable than their competitors.

Universities aren't only Big Data producers nowadays; they're also institutions more and more conditioned by Big Data itself. Indeed, metrics and measurement govern academic knowledge production and the delivery of teaching quality. Numbers drive a target culture that dominates academic life almost everywhere. Higher education is a huge knowledge economy, a diverse business of applied expertise and vocational training. Research is increasingly geared towards economic innovation, and teaching seems valued only insofar as it prepares young people for the professional labour market.

Performance is kept up to speed through endless assessments and target settings, inaugurated in Britain by Tony Blair's New Labour government after it came to power in 1997. In 1998, New Labour set Britain apart from continental Europe and abandoned free higher education, introducing a tuition fee system for undergraduates. Framing education very much in terms of economic neoliberalism, a decade later they acted on the basis of a 2010 White Paper called 'Securing a Sustainable Future for Higher Education', and slashed almost all public funding from higher-education teaching.

'Securing a Sustainable Future for Higher Education' was produced by a panel of independent 'experts' convened by Lord Browne, a businessman with little university sector experience, Sir Michael Barber, a Blairite education pundit, and a team of McKinsey management consultants. Their recommendations set university administrators the task of replacing lost income themselves. Rather than hobble along as sluggish statist behemoths, the Browne Report insisted, universities need to become competitive entrepreneurial corporations, standing on their own two feet. Being reliant on government for all teaching income 'reduces universities' responsiveness to students'.

Universities should innovate economically, the Report said, embrace new technology, such as MOOCs (massively open online courses, the 'next big thing' in university life),[6] and rebrand themselves to fit specific market 'niches'. They need to 'unbundle' their functions, delivering teaching in a number of comparatively advantageous areas rather than in all areas. Students are fee-paying consumers now, who have choices in an educational market. They'll increasingly see higher education as an investment and go searching for the least expensive course to help them get the highest-paying professional job. Competition between universities will eventually cheapen the costs of education, while at the same time improving its quality. Or so the reasoning goes.

To ensure the quality of educational output – on both teaching and research flanks – obligatory audits and assessments have resulted in escalating managerialism and professionalisation. The main measure of UK scholarly output these days is another New Labour invention: the 'Research Excellence Framework' (REF), a discipline-based audit, undertaken by academics themselves. Occurring every five years or so, scholarly 'output' – peer-reviewed articles, books, chapters in edited books – is measured and assessed, totted up and ranked on a scale of 1 to 4 in terms of its 'impact'. Impact means 'usefulness' for outside society, relevance to wider social concerns, to public health and public services, to environmental and economic life.

Of course, the question of just what 'impact' and 'usefulness' means, and how it's decided, is bureaucratically time-consuming as well as ever more costly (the 2014 REF was estimated to have set universities back a collective total of £246 million, compared with £66 million for the previous research assessment in 2008). The REF is nothing short of a massive and tyrannical data-gathering sweep. Yet it's vital for academic departments, because government research grant money is dished out on the basis of highest-impacting departments. League tables are constructed therefrom. Universities are encouraged to build upon their successes and ditch their failures.

Invariably, Big Data STEM subjects (Science, Technology, Engineering and Mathematics) gain better citation scores, counting for more because they matter more to business, to the private sector, to boosting economic productivity. On the other hand, non-STEM humanities and social science disciplines usually have less impact and lower citation indices. Crucially, too, they're less likely to receive lavish external grant money. The downgrading of purely intellectual or politically critical research is one perpetual shortcoming in a strange looping argument that suggests to improve education you need to fix targets to show improvement; but when you do this you find an education system geared to achieving targets and little else. The 'metrics tide', as some have called it,[7] flows like a torrent of peer-reviewed journals weighted for their specific impact factor. They're now effectively a proxy to assess an academic's output, his or her research 'quality'.

Little wonder the symbiosis between academics' frantic need to publish and the academic publishing industry, eager to accumulate capital. Hence the reams of articles churned out by the academic sausage factory. And hence the enormous growth of peer-reviewed scholarly journals run by multinational publishing conglomerates, a massive online and offline industry. Science, technical and medical articles alone generate $9.4 billion in revenue for the English-language publishing industry. In 2013, an analysis of 45 million articles indexed in the Web of Science revealed that just five publishing companies control 70 per cent of global output: Reed-Elsevier, Springer, Wiley-Blackwell, Taylor & Francis, and Sage. Reed-Elsevier, one of the most predatory, gleaned $1.5

billion during the first half of 2014 for its scientific, medical and technical journals. For some of its publications, the company charges dependent authors to appear in their 'professional' pages. Upon acceptance of a manuscript, a scholar is duly invoiced. In a way, it's a double whammy for academics: to publish or perish, *and* pay for the privilege.

But what does impact really mean here, beyond a guide for self-referential academe, where inner circles emerge and friends reciprocally cite one another? The greater the number of citations, the greater the scholarship. That's how it goes. Certain indexes become the basis for tenure and promotion, for grants and fellowships, for illustrious invitations and visiting chairs. In today's marketplace of ideas, the citation is a unit of currency, a Visa card to scholarly success, measuring not the quality of one's work but the size of one's network: the scope of connections to people in high places, to journal editors and professional paradigm gatekeepers.

You can classify and measure anything you like, using any yardstick you like, to obtain the results and ordering you wanted all along. That's why there's a selected arbitrariness and circularity about a system that lives and dies by metrics. Applied to education, it's a vision that the radical pedagogue Ivan Illich, in his counter-metrics manifesto *Deschooling Society*, called '*irrational consistency*'. Irrational consistency arises whenever the 'cult of efficiency' strikes. 'Irrational consistency mesmerises accomplices who are engaged in mutually expedient and disciplined exploitation. It's a logic', Illich says, 'generated by bureaucratic behaviour';[8] a system of classification that bases itself on a 'rationality' serving the interests of those who created the classification criteria in the first place. For Illich, this is the most sinister form of rationality because it sounds utterly logical and disciplined, a taxonomy that's highly consistent in its irrationality. To illustrate his point, Illich turns to the Argentinian scribe Jorge Luis Borges, a wizard of confounding labyrinths, who evokes the sense of giddiness associated with irrational consistency.

In the early 1940s, Borges wrote 'The Analytical Language of John Wilkins', a short essay about a real-life seventeenth-century English scholar obsessed with encyclopaedic classification. On the face of it, Borges's piece is straight-laced, but there's an undertow of black humour. Wilkins had variously been an archbishop, the warden of Oxford's Wadham College, the master of Cambridge's Trinity College, and the first secretary of the Royal Society. He was a polymath absorbed by linguistics, astronomy, theology, music and cryptography. Borges tells us how Wilkins toyed with the idea of building a transparent beehive and explored the possibility of a trip to the moon, even of orbiting an invisible planet. His lifelong passion, however, was to develop the principles of a universal language, a language organised to cover *all* human ideas and categories, divided and subdivided using symbols and lettering, analytically categorised, consistently worked out – if we accept the logic of Wilkins's own head.

Borges observes that 'the analytical language of Wilkins is not the least admirable ... the artifice of using the letters of the words to indicate divisions and subdivisions is undoubtedly ingenious.' And yet, for all that, 'I have registered the arbitrariness of Wilkins.' 'The classes and species that compose it are contradictory and vague'. His system is brilliant but 'full of conjecture', simply because there's no system of classification that isn't full of conjecture, no taxonomy that doesn't come into being because *somebody* feels it can serve their purpose: their taxonomy *must* make sense, 'the same way', Illich adds, that 'the taxonomy of educational objectives makes sense to scientific authors'.

The latest taxonomy proposed by British higher education elites was outlined in a Conservative government Green Paper, 'Fulfilling Our Potential: Teaching Excellence, Social Mobility and Student Choice' (November 2015). Therein a 'Teaching Excellence Framework' (TEF) is unveiled, a pedagogic parallel to the REF. Yet another expert panel of representatives – from employers, professional groups, senior academics and student bodies – is set to design and develop a new curriculum in which graduates 'can contribute more effectively to our efforts to boost the productivity of the UK economy'.[9] Now, universities should be 'open to involving employers and learned societies representing professions in curriculum design', cultivating 'a positive work ethic'. 'Prospective students will be able to use TEF results to help inform their decisions about which institutions to attend, and employers can consider it in their recruitment.'

The Green Paper identified that three years after graduating, some 20 per cent of STEM graduates aren't working in jobs that match their skills and qualifications; worse, many non-STEM graduates are unemployed. So there's a 'mismatch', which is undermining the economy. This challenge will be addressed by making universities more vocational, more like professional preparatory centres, training young people, equipping them with the skills they'll need to become successful professionals. Degrees will be tantamount to apprenticeships. Indeed, the Green Paper touts a category of 'degree apprentice', a student who'll 'be employed throughout [their studies] and so have the opportunity to develop skills directly required by employers'. Plausible metrics will doubtless be found to measure the quality and relevance of teaching; universities will brand themselves accordingly, on the basis of relevance scores and cost competitiveness.

There is good cause to fear that universities will tailor themselves even more to corporate models, cost-cutting where they can. And as all good corporations discover in aggressive market situations, the handiest victim is labour costs, resulting in a drift towards increasing casualisation: temporary teaching contracts, contracts for teaching specific courses, piecemeal, paid by the hour, with no security, no benefits, no dignity. Whether such a model is ever going to produce 'excellence' remains to be seen.

I guess it boils down to what you mean by 'excellence'. The US, as ever, sets the tone, since it has 'successfully' squared the circle, reconciling the high bar of excellence with the low bar of casualisation. The American Association of University Professors suggests that some 76 per cent of college and university academics aren't either tenured or following any tenure track. They're completely insecure – a smart contingent labour force.

Job insecurity is one of the biggest concerns amongst British academics. In 2015, the *Times Higher Education* polled 2,900 higher educational staff, from all ranks and roles, working in 150 institutions across the country, in its third annual 'University Workplace Study'.[10] The majority of British academics now believe metrics-based performance measures will lead to more redundancies. 'University leadership are on record saying they want a high staff turnover', one academic is quoted as saying, 'and [pursue] this perverse aim by setting unreasonable personal targets for all academic staff, enforcing them with a new draconian performance assessment system.' 'We are being set funding targets which, it is widely acknowledged,' another says, 'are impossible for even half of us to meet. The sense among many of us is that this is the first step in a process of [constructive] dismissal.' Still another admits: 'My work at my university feels highly stressful and insecure.' 'Now it is all about metrics. Performance management is really a euphemism for: "If we don't like you, we will get rid of you."'

For a while, I thought academia might be a good way-station for someone like me, an oddball amateur. I thought it might be a route to having a real job that wasn't a real job. I thought that maybe there I could transmit my passion for books and ideas to younger people without having to disguise it, all the while getting paid for it. You know, like being an amateur with a profession. But I was wrong. It never worked out for me, despite being dedicated to what I did. I worked hard, reading and writing, planning my classes, contriving new ways to stimulate myself and my students. I assigned books that had touched me and which I hoped would touch others: *Notes from Underground*, *All That Is Solid Melts into Air*, *Social Justice and the City*, *Capital*, *Death and Life of Great American Cities*, *Paris Spleen*, *Ulysses*, *The Society of the Spectacle*. I was into the purity of the content and was good at conveying it. I never needed much money to do my writing or teaching. On the contrary, I would have done it all for nothing.

At first, I thought this was a plus; I was cheap, had no overheads, was low-budget, with high output. I thought I could just get on with what excited me. What I wrote and taught seemed one and the same. I had a life in books and put books back into life. I never had to travel much, either; never really wanted to. My research was local, based on where and how I lived, yet global, too, framed by a wider realm of experience, experience gained by experience. I wanted to be a 'spiritual citizen of the universe', in the poet Baudelaire's words, and help others become one as well. But hard work without research money counted for nothing: I had no impact, my metrics were bad, I couldn't quantify what I did, measure anything. I was no expert.

I even began to think as one of my heroes, Guy Debord, had thought: 'Of course, if one contemplates not my emoluments but only my abilities, no one can doubt that I have been a very good professional. But in what domain?' If anything, my teaching was anti-vocational. I taught young kids to think critically about the world and their place in it, to make them wary of the neoliberal labour market they'd have to confront. I wanted them to know that professionalism was a lie and a ruse, so beware. My ideal of academia was increasingly anti-academia, swimming against the metrics tide. I knew then it was time to get out of the water.

Twenty-five years ago, I remember starting my first job, at the University of Southampton. I'd taken up the post while completing my doctorate. It seemed like a good opportunity. But it came right on the heels of my time as a grad student, a formative time. I'd been so stimulated at Oxford that most nights, my head abuzz with ideas, I barely slept. I felt like Stephen Dedalus, in Joyce's *Portrait of the Artist as a Young Man*: 'His soul was swooning into some new world, fantastic, dim, uncertain as under sea, traversed by cloudy shapes and beings.' I'd had an impassioned amateur experience, belonging to a small cohort of independent fellow-travellers centred around David Harvey.

Before that it had been Trevor Jones at Liverpool Poly, and his cough-ball laughter. In the twilight of his career, Trevor was an amateur slowly getting swallowed up by professionals. Many senior Poly administrators saw him as a wastrel, a corrupting influence on young minds. In action, Trevor was a sight to behold. Short and thin, with rotten teeth, dishevelled hair and a pot belly about the size of a football – hastened by years of steady libation – he paced up and down the classroom, rolling a cigarette, smoking his pathetic butt, puffing and pausing, thinking and talking. He spoke in an inimitably breezy tone – laconic, slightly mocking, mischievously derisive of bourgeois values and professional pretensions.

Trevor also taught off campus, as it were, drinking with everybody and anybody. He led me into a whole new mode of existence, down through the circles of Liverpool's urban inferno into the shady world of penniless literati, artists and writers, actors and wannabes, men and women of ideas – some authentic, some posturing, and some untalented and on the dole. All hung out in smoky downtown pubs, bars and coffee shops, where proletarian wisdom got produced and circulated like a species of educational metrics way off the official charts. There, Plato, Marx and Freud met Bill Shankly and the Fab Four. Dialogues were usually smart yet vulgar, intellectual yet loud, rigorous yet heated – profane truths – as juices flowed and tempers flared. I'd found a new, wild life singing in my veins.

But when I began at Southampton as a paid professional, a junior lecturer, everything went flat and lifeless; the listlessness was contagious; the sensibility was sensible. There was little intellectual stimulation, and very few characters. A lot of my fifty-something colleagues were merely going through the motions, dreaming of imminent retirement. They were straight and always would be. They'd not published anything for years, save a few book reviews back in the 1970s. They seemed more preoccupied with repairing ruined French châteaus than with revamping yellowing course notes.

They were giving professionals a bad name, a bad reputation. Even to a naïve rookie like me it was obvious that something needed to be done. Universities felt stale and mouldy; morale was low. These demoralised lecturers were the non-performing tail of a beast that was soon to undergo metamorphosis. They needed to be purged: they were poor teachers and desultory writers. Making academia more go-getting, more entrepreneurial, even, didn't seem such a bad idea back then. What could be the harm in a greater connection with public affairs and the outside world? After all, jobs and labour markets were changing, so why should academia be any different? Why shouldn't it have its 'halo' removed, like other professions? Change in academia was necessary. But what kind, and to what end?

It's clear that the bathwater needed draining. But now that it's gone, what's left? The baby? Was there really ever any baby in academia? At any rate, the waters have now parted – between academics and administrators, between their artisanal labour process and the increasingly distant professional apparatus that controls it. Most academics these days never stop working. They can't. They're permanently online, terrified to log off. In that *Times Higher Education* Workplace Survey, excessive work hours were highlighted as a major problem for academics. 'I feel unappreciated', one commented. 'I work 100 hours a week and I'm exhausted.' 'The workload is unimaginable', another said. 'I work unspeakable hours.' Fully 68 per cent said they work too much, every weekend and often on Christmas Day. 'I don't think I can realistically keep this up until retirement without making myself seriously ill from stress.'

Looking back, I see that my own learning experience flourished in the interregnum of the 1980s, in a strange interstitial time and space, in the ruins of an older age, before the Phoenix of a newer had arisen. I was lucky: it became something positive amid a lot of negativity and turmoil, especially political turmoil. When I finally got around to going to college, I discovered that Margaret Thatcher's government was beginning to take apart the public sector that had enabled me to go there. In Liverpool, anti-Thatcher sentiment was tangled up with what was happening locally.

Between 1983 and 1987, a hard-core 'entryist' faction of the Labour Party called Militant controlled the city council, a fiercely anti-Thatcher, Trotskyist 'party within a Party'. (It was fiercely anti-Labour, too, frequently clashing with Neil Kinnock's revisionism.) By the mid-1980s, the entire public sector in Liverpool seemed to be on strike. That's how I remember it, anyway. The Poly entrance along Tithebarn Street was usually blockaded, classes cancelled. I didn't know it then, but I was getting an offsite (and offside) extra-curricular education, learning urban theory and politics in the field, on the street. It was even the kind of *deschooling* experience that Ivan Illich portrays in his ground-breaking yet woefully ignored book, one that will never feature in any education White Paper.

In the early 1960s, Illich had established the Centro Intercultural de Documentación (CIDOC), a language and research centre, a free university in an old hacienda at Cuernavaca, south of Mexico City. There, he taught and dialogued with everybody and anybody: with do-good missionaries and hippie misfits, with drop-outs and emissaries; soon enough he'd have them all denouncing US imperialism and capitalist industrial development, questioning professional technocracy and actually existing democracy. CIDOC's radicalism and independent thinkery attracted streams of converts, inspired by Illich's boundless energy and convivial spirit.

In *Deschooling Society*, a text that emerged from those CIDOC years, Illich said that students in the US and Europe are 'schooled' into confusing classrooms with learning, grade advancement with education, a diploma with competence. 'Bureaucracies claim professional, political and financial monopoly over the social imagination,' he reckoned, 'setting standards of what is valuable and what is feasible.' The values educational institutions instil 'are quantified ones'. They initiate young people into a world where everything can be measured, 'including their imaginations, and, indeed, man himself'. But personal development, Illich insisted, 'isn't a measurable entity. It is growth in disciplined dissidence, which cannot be measured against any rod, or any curriculum, nor compared to someone else's achievements.'

Illich is dead against educational programmes that funnel students into narrowly defined professional roles. That's what he means by being 'schooled down to size'. It's not the best way to stand tall. And it's not the best way to liberate the creative resources within people. It's not that education shouldn't be geared towards contributing to society or to the economy. What's problematic today is how withered the vision of this preparation is. To educate, says Illich, is to 'liberate the individual from the obligation to shape his or her expectations to the services offered by an established profession'.

That's why I consider myself as deschooled: I learned how to unlearn, and continue to follow the twisted path of 'disciplined dissidence'. All I did as an academic was pass on to students the immeasurable joy of what had been passed on to me.

4

City of Amateurs

Growing up in Liverpool has taught me that cities are part and parcel of the educational process, that they are places where ordinary people can learn about life – sometimes the hard way. My own immersion in books has been so deeply bound up with my immersion in cities that it's hard to differentiate the two. The arrows flow in both directions, informing one another, fuelling one another. I understood early on what the great urbanist and essayist Walter Benjamin meant when he was unpacking his library: each book on the shelf, he said, was like a little memento of a time spent wandering the streets, a tiny brick with which he could reconstruct past urban environments and perhaps even imagine new ones to come. 'How many cities have revealed themselves to me in the marches I undertook in the pursuit of books!'[1]

Benjamin was talking about seeking out books by seeking out gem bookstores, used and independent, which invariably reveal gem parts of the city, used parts of the city, lived in and well thumbed. Bookstores are signposts that have led me on many voyages of discovery, helping me unearth unknown neighbour-hoods and unexpected street-corner societies. In our own times, I tend to think of independent bookstores as something of a canary in a coal mine, the last gasp of a breathable air that hasn't been poisoned by fracked economic value. If they survive, there's a good chance that the neighbourhood, too, survives, preserving its affordability, its mixed use, its mixed population. I've known plenty of bookstores that survive by forever moving on – being forever *moved on* – constantly upping sticks, reclaiming cheaper or abandoned spaces, usually further out on the edge; sometimes they become the magnet for new, emergent neighbourhoods in the ruins, out on a periphery that might one day reassert itself more centrally. The dynamic geography of bookstores is but a map of changing city land and lease values.

My romance with books has, in short, been a romance with the city. For me, it was the Beats who best staked out this terrain in the 1950s. 'Beat', Kerouac once said, 'meaning down and out but full of intense conviction … a new generation of men and women intent on joy.' 'Live your life out? Naw, *love* your life out.' I still find the Beats and their works inspiring, even as I read them in middle age. The cheap thrills of the city were their muse: jazz clubs (when they were still cheap), streets, ordinary workaday cafeterias, sitting around Formica tables drinking coffee, discoursing about Dostoevsky and Nietzsche, literature and existential angst, while generally goofing around. 'Goofing at the table', declaims Kerouac in one of his 'blues' poems. 'You just don't know – "What don't I know?" – How good this ham 'n eggs is. If you had any idea whatsoever how good this is, then you would stop writing poetry and dig in. It's been so long since I have been hungry, it's like a miracle.'

It was this miracle of the everyday city that Robert Frank documented in his debut 'Beat' film, the twenty-eight minute *Pull My Daisy* (1959), scripted, with an ad-lib narration, by Jack Kerouac. Beat poets Allen Ginsberg and Gregory Corso 'star', playing themselves in an improvised alchemy that relives scenes from the ordinary madness of the life of Neal Cassady (Dean Moriarty in *On the Road*) with his wife Carolyn Robinson. Frank said the film 'was made by non-professionals in search of that freer vision'.[2] Kerouac said to him, in his introduction to Frank's great photography book *The Americans*, 'You got eyes.' I still remember why I loved *Pull My Daisy*: it was a snapshot of how I wanted to live, how I wanted to *be* in the city.

This impulse was a city of poets who were ordinary people and ordinary people who were poets, living in grungy affordability, a life that mixes the epic and the artistic – the late-night parties, the jam sessions, the beautiful sociability of fellow-travellers, the coffee houses and bookstores, Ginsberg and Corso arguing about Apollinaire – with the everyday familial. The film begins with a panned shot of a Bowery loft, adorned with paintings, shelves full of books and bohemian curios; artist mother, Carolyn – played by the only 'professional' actor in the crew, Delphine Seyrig – pulls back the shutters, breakfasts, and readies son Pablo (Frank's own son) for school, 'early morning in the universe', says Kerouac.

Almost all of *Pull My Daisy* takes place within the apartment's interior. But the most arresting scene is one of the few exteriors: a misty shot, glimpsed through the apartment window, of Carolyn and Pablo holding hands down below on the sidewalk, trying to cross over a busy Fourth Avenue, dancing and hopping merrily, son swinging around mom. Pablo waves up at Frank's camera, and, with touching melancholy, Kerouac's voiceover sounds: '… got to go to school, to learn all about geography and astromomology and tripeology and all them ologies, and poetology and goodbyeology … goodbye …'

This street scene could have easily taken place on the other side of town, the West Side in Greenwich Village, where just then another savvy urbanist with eyes was producing her own artistic oeuvre: *The Death and Life of Great American Cities*. It was Jane Jacobs, of course; and Carolyn and Pablo were participating in what she'd call 'the intricate sidewalk ballet'. 'Although it is life, not art,' Jacobs says,

> we may fancifully call it the art of the city and liken it to the dance – not to a simple-minded precision dance with everyone kicking up at the same time, twirling in unison and bowing off en masse, but to an intricate ballet in which individual dancers and ensembles all have distinctive parts which miraculously reinforce each other and compose an orderly whole. The ballet of the city sidewalk never repeats itself from place to place, and in any one place is always replete with new impro-visations.[3]

Each day, the ballet along Hudson Street, Jacobs says, 'eddies back and forth with intricate vigour'. It starts out early, with the familiar 'rituals of morning': Carolyn and Pablo walking to school; Mr Halpert, a Jacobian everyman, unlocking the laundry's handcart; Joe Cornacchia stacking out empty crates from his delicatessen; Mr Goldstein opening his hardware store. Later, the 'heart-of-the-day ballet' mixes familiar faces with those of strangers, the office and meat-market workers filling the bakery lunchroom, longshoremen hitting the bars, young and old bohemians and students hanging out, women pushing baby carriages, the myriad passers-by going about their business. The ballet reaches 'its crescendo' as kids quit school and 'clusters of everyone from toddlers with dolls to teen-agers with homework gather at the stoops'. As darkness strikes, the 'deep night ballet' unfolds, and other 'character dances' come on, some rowdy and jubilant, others sad and lonely. Bars fill up, night workers stop off at the delicatessen for milk and salami: 'Things have settled down for the evening but the street and its ballet have not come to a stop.'[4]

Jacobs's delight is for what Marshall Berman liked to call 'the primal symbol of modern life': the city street, microcosmic public spaces that constitute the macrocosmic urban totality, that give it its life-blood, that keep it pulsating. But the kind of street Jacobs affirms is the busy street that harbours many uses, that melds with a housing stock that folk of modest means can afford. Jacobs eyes the city with a richer texturing, seeing things that planners and professionals refused to see, couldn't see: from the bottom upwards, from the standpoint of the ordinary, from the standpoint of a woman. Planners sought order for the sake of simplification, hacking into the old city, razing vast tracts, demolishing and renewing, breaking things up by zoning things out; but Jacobs marvelled at the 'organised complexity' of disorder, the hurly-burly that made people want to come to the city and linger.

She wrote about cities lovingly and compellingly, even while fiercely dismissing the professionals who stood in her way, who somehow towered over her. With *Death and Life of Great American Cities*, ordinary people were handed a powerful field manual to counter professional pronouncements about urban development. With its catalogue of workaday folk on old street blocks, Jacobs offered a vision of the city that let common citizens recognise themselves as city makers, not simply city users, and see their real place in urban life, perhaps for the first time.

If hers was the kind of city I wanted to live in, hers was a method of studying cities I also wanted to follow. It was low-budget, no-thrills, qualitative and subjective, earthy and commonsensical – amateurish, we might say – based on somewhere nearby. The experience of the city isn't reducible to a counting game, to statistics and population densities, to something read off the census or 'officially' mapped. There's a lot more going on, Jacobs revealed, a lot more *there* there.

Jacobs had an important admirer and significant supporter: William H. 'Holly' Whyte, another thorn in the side of conventionality. Early on, Whyte had commissioned Jacobs to write a major piece on cities for *Fortune* magazine, where he worked as an editor. 'She came through', Whyte said, 'with a slashing attack on current planning dogma, a spirited affirmation of the street that it scorned, and shortly thereafter went on to develop the themes of her classic *Death and Life of Great American Cities*.' The *Fortune* article, 'Downtown Is for People', appeared in April 1958. It's still one of the finest standalone essays ever written about cities, and it provides great clues to what an amateur urbanism might consist of.[5]

'There's no logic that can be superimposed on the city', Jacobs says. 'People make it, and it is to them, not buildings, that we must fit our plans.' Professionals must follow, must respond to amateurs – not the other way around. 'The citizen should be the ultimate expert', argues Jacobs. 'What is needed is an observant eye, curiosity about people, and a willingness to walk … Let the citizens decide what end results they want, and they can adapt the rebuilding machinery to suit them. If new laws are needed, they can agitate to get them… What a wonderful challenge there is! Rarely before has the citizen had such a chance to reshape the city, and to make it the kind of city that they like and that others will too. If this means leaving room for the incongruous, or the vulgar or the strange, that is part of the challenge, not the problem'.

For his part, fellow-traveller 'Holly' Whyte had written a best-selling book in the mid-1950s, *The Organization Man*, which took apart the 'groupthink' of American corporate culture. Whyte challenged the idea that big business was daring and entrepreneurial; it was quite the reverse, he said, more about 'organisational crawl', about bureaucracies pursuing safety and security, controlled not by pioneering risk-takers but by suburban executives with conservative aspirations. The same deadening conformity, Whyte foresaw in the 1960s, was deadening cities, too; Jacobs would be the first to concur.

In the early 1970s, Whyte formed a small research group in New York called The Street Life Project, and began looking closely at city spaces – at public spaces. As he pointed out, hitherto simple observation had been used only by anthropologists and ethnographers in far-off lands, for the understanding of exotic cultures. It hadn't been adopted to look at city life close at hand, in commonplace modern spaces. So, like a traditional ethnographer, Whyte sat down to observe for long periods, watching city life go by, recording what he saw with pen and paper, documenting 'the social life of small urban spaces'.[6] Clipboard in hand, Whyte dutifully recorded the physical and social landscape of urban America. He also set up a series of time-lapse cameras on and above the street, speeding the pedestrian flow, the chance encounters, the human-scale activity that unfolded on the street, in parks and plazas, outside subway stations.[7]

Whyte discovered why some public spaces worked and others didn't, why some attracted crowds while others discouraged them. He produced charts, diagrams and a few metrics of his own: indexes and maps of jaywalkers and jaytalkers, of people lingering, of people watching people, of people eating, of people doing nothing in the midst of people. 'What attracts people most', Whyte concludes, in his homily about which public spaces work best, 'is other people.' 'Lovers are found in plazas', he notes. 'But not where you'd expect them. The most fervent embracing we've recorded has usually taken place in the visible locations with the couple oblivious of the crowd.'

> People tend to sit most where there are places to sit. This may not strike you as an intellectual bombshell, and, now that I look back on our study, I wonder why it was not more apparent from the beginning ... Ideally, sitting should be physically comfortable – benches with back rests, well-contoured chairs. It's more important, however, that it be *socially* comfortable. This means choice: sitting up front, in the back, to the side, in the sun, in the shade, in groups, off alone.

Whyte's special affection is for street vendors. He advocates food kiosks and snack bars with plenty of tables and chairs, because if you want to seed a place for activity, he says, 'put out food'. 'Vendors have a good nose for spaces that work.' They introduce a figure Whyte calls a 'mayor', somebody who spends all day in the space, keeping an eye on things, making people feel comfortable. Alas, 'the civic establishment deplores all this', Whyte says. 'There are enough ordinances to make it illegal for vendors, licensed or not, to do business at any spot where business is good.' The cops do periodic sweeps, arriving in trucks to haul the vendors away. But the vendor 'fills a void', says Whyte, 'and this can become quite clear when he's shooed away. A lot of the life of the space goes with him.'

Whyte, like Jacobs, loves the messy agora: the crowded public square, the congested city street. He's all for 'self-congestion', too, which, he believes, is a primal impulse of urban dwellers – notwithstanding professionals who think otherwise. Like Jacobs, Whyte was an educator and an agitator: he mobilised low-budget research for high-level action, lobbying City Hall, frequently shaming planners, architects and developers into installing more accessible public space. Whyte was firmly against the tokenism of 'incentive zoning', where developers boost their commercial space by tacking on a bit of public space in some gloomy, secluded court-yard that nobody can find. For Whyte as for Jacobs, the genius of the city, its true colours, is its most ancient ideal: that it's a place where people can come together face-to-face, walk and mingle, meet and argue and become a public who's present in the creation of its own urbanity.

Masterplans instigated by public planning authorities are no longer the stake in urban issues. That battle has largely been won. Public planners and strategic regulatory bodies seem relics today of a bygone age of city development. By the time we entered the 1990s, the dominant paradigm had shifted away from the public towards the private, away from urban managerialism towards urban cor-poratism. The large-scale razing and renewal that Jacobs railed against is no longer a danger. If anything, the threat is subtler: professional urbanists and developers, architects and designers now speak Jacobs's own language. They give their projects a 'Janewash', a veneer of community involving street fiestas, creative classes and bohemian spaces, high densities and walkabilities. The trouble is that a lot of this sneaks in under the banner of free-market economics whose outcomes are soaring rents, gentrification and displacement.

Cities have always been about big business and big bucks, of course. Now, though, it's big business and big bucks with a few twists and turns. The urban landscape has broadened; prospects for profitability and patronage have expanded. The global reach of cities has been empirically proven by urban experts and pro-fessionals. Since 2006, the United Nations Human Settlement

Program (UN-Habitat) tells us that the balance has tipped: the majority of the world's inhabitants, some 3.3 billion people, live in urban agglomerations, not rural areas. By 2030, it's set to be 4.9 billion, around 60 per cent of the world's population. By then, an extra 590,000 square miles of the planet will have been urbanised, spelling an additional 1.47 billion urban denizens. If the trend continues, by 2050, 75 per cent of planet Earth will be urbanised.

Ours is an 'Urban Age', an epoch that's been a veritable field day for professional do-gooders and go-getters, for experts and specialists who plead for the poor while placating the rich – those big funders and grant givers, the wealthy foundations and billionaire philanthropists. It's led to a primitive accumulation of expert knowledge that now sets the agenda in debates around our urban future. The study of cities is a thriving business that boosts professional careers as well as personal bank balances. There's been plenty of rehearsed gabbing, and the promise of high-profile, canned TEDx appearances has lured impact-seeking academics and ambitious professionals into taking the shilling, into driving a juicy new growth sector: *urban solutionism*.

Solutionism invariably gravitates between *triumphalism* and *dystopianism*. On the one hand is *triumphalism*, a celebration of our new urban order, flogging the belief that cities hold the key to global economic well-being, indeed are the very motors of this well-being, 'productive' engines in their own right. (80 per cent of global GDP, triumphalists aver, is generated by cities.) Consequently, urban solutionism needs to nurture and maximise this capacity.

The most triumphal of the triumphalists is Harvard University's urban free-marketeer, Edward Glaeser, whose bestselling *Triumph of the City* staked out the pathway to our future urban success. The city is a triumph to behold and to be extolled, Glaeser says.

Human capital is the solution, a factor of production to be tapped; cities have agglomerations of it. Cities need to foster high-rise living, augment the clustered density of people. It's an economics of scale that promotes innovation, a vertical densification of the city and of economic possibility. Building height restrictions need to be eliminated, says Glaeser, and regulations that hobble free-market competition must be loosened. Develop freer institutions, ditch preservation statutes and zoning laws, ditch the public sector altogether. Housing, Glaeser contends, will then become more abundant and hence more affordable. The city will flourish, entrepreneurship will triumph through urban free-market therapy; trickle-down will enable everyone to share in its rewards.[8]

A similar line is peddled by another urban triumphalist, Richard Florida, the director of the University of Toronto's Martin Prosperity Institute. Since *The Rise of the Creative Class*, Florida has become a one-man start-up company who's turned his 'creative class' concept into a global export conglomerate, an advertisement for his real product: himself, the paradigmatic urban solutions consultant. Florida has developed all kinds of indices and metrics to show how cities with vibrant neighbourhoods and buoyant economies tend to contain above-average bohemian, techie, artistic and gay populations. The most dynamic and commercially successful cities thus have young, smart, highly-educated professionals – the vaunted 'creative classes' – bundled together on the same patch, mingling together, riffing on one another.[9]

Such innovatory capacity, for Florida, becomes a salutary 'solution', meaning that people in urban power should cater to these groups by offering incentives and inducements to let them create more. The fruits accruing therefrom will, again, trickle down to the less hip, less smart or less able. And in the meantime, says Florida, urban spaces will get more 'vibrant' and after a while vibrancy will economically fuel itself. Like Glaeser, Florida thinks that 'zoning restrictions make segregation worse'. They limit housing construction, thus bottlenecking supply and raising costs all round. It follows that authorities should lift restrictions and let the private sector build more housing for the rich (and for the creative classes), rather than more affordable housing, because, says Florida, the poor will ultimately be better off that way.[10]

Glaeser and Florida are terrific fans of Jane Jacobs, and both acknowledge their professional debt to our most popular amateur urbanist. Yet what they see as 'triumphs' of the city work against the sort of diversity that Jacobs extolled. Free-market triumphs have helped destroy the mixed land-uses and organised complexity she singled out as the most important ingredient of a vibrant city life. Jacobs said city blocks 'need high-yield, middling-yield, low-yield, and no-yield enterprises'.[11]

But cities these days are arenas for high-yields only, for gleaning land rent, for making property pay any way it can, where people are priced off the land through the private appropriation of space. Rich people and rich companies see city real estate and central locations as ever more profitable, relatively risk-free, financial investments. In the mix there's not much mix: prominent city spaces become functionally and financially standardised. There might be techno-hipsters based there, a Google or a Zappos, a Cisco or a McKinsey; there might, too, be experimental spaces and creative hubs and creative classes; yet there's a common thrust throughout – to exploit the business potential of every nook and cranny of urban life.[12]

The economies of the world's biggest metropolises are increasingly predicated on extractive activity, which, through the normal operation of their land and housing markets, decant non-profit-maximising activities, together with less solvent people, to some other part of town, usually way out on the periphery. Privatisation and market rationality in urban life have become orthodoxies that cut across political parties as well as national boundaries, engineered and endorsed seemingly everywhere by assorted real-estate professionals, architects, business chiefs, start-up CEOs and government officials, all of whom appear content to go with the free market flow.

This is part of the rationale for that other strand of the Urban Age, its less boosterish face: *dystopianism*. Here again, of course, professionals stalk the corridors of power, scaremongering for funds and fulminating against the Sodoms and Gomorrahs in our midst. Neo-Malthusian arguments prevail: urban regions are just too big, too over-populated, too threatening, too environmentally hazardous. Cities wallow in excrement and decay, pollution and squalor; they have too many people for the available resources. Hence the plethora of professional agencies and institutes, supra-national foundations and non-profits, that want to 'help' – by proposing private-sector-led partnerships to assist the tired and huddled masses.

They dream up vast new infrastructure projects and fresh technological fixes. They seem to want to do everything except attack property speculation and impugn the market; they refuse to acknowledge resource scarcity as the socially produced reality it is, artificially created, defined through access to wealth and monopoly power. Professional dystopians bemoan scarcity while professional triumphalists squander 'scarce' resources, pouring them into edifices built by 'starchitects' like Frank Gehry or Renzo Piano or Rem Koolhaas. All this at a time when the public sector is under fire from austerity. Triumphalism and dystopianism thus feed off each other, actively necessitate each other. They're different sides of the same professional urban coin. Either way, what we have here is a new deadening conformity to the current order, a flattening of the city, not an enrichment of it.

One of the best known 'Urban Age' initiatives straddles this triumphalist-dystopian dialectic, wriggles between its terms: the eponymous programme engineered by Ricky Burdett at the London School of Economics (LSE). Burdett is an urban professional with fingers in many pies; notwithstanding the programme's broadly leftist good intentions, he runs as merrily with the hounds as with the hares. He holds chairs at Harvard's Graduate School of Design and New York University, and was chief advisor on architecture and urbanism for London's 2012 Olympics. With former *Observer* architecture critic Deyan Sudjic, current director of London's Design Museum, Burdett has edited two glossy showpieces, *The Endless City* (2005) and *Living in the Endless City* (2011). Architects Richard Rogers and Norman Foster are Urban Age associates; ditto UN-Habitat boss Joan Clos, a former mayor of Barcelona. It's a cosy, elite affair, with further intellectual muscle supplied by globetrotting husband and wife duo Richard Sennett and Saskia Sassen.

Every year the Deutsche Bank sponsors the LSE's Urban Age Award, a competition between cities worth $100k. For our professional types *love* competitions: architecture and art competitions, biennale prizes, competitions for who's the best at whatnot. The Urban Age Award is presented 'to initiatives within a specific city that utilise partnerships to improve the quality of life and the quality of the urban environment'. It was 'created to encourage people to take responsibility for their cities and form new alliances'. Former recipients include teams from Mumbai, São Paulo, Istanbul, Mexico City, Cape Town, Rio and New Delhi. 'Those who want to shape the future', we hear, 'must also shape our cities.'

In early 2016, LSE's Urban Age co-led a special United Cities and Local Governments (UCLG) initiative, 'a group of twenty global experts' convening around a preparatory process for UN-Habitat (III). Their mission is to develop a 'New Urban Agenda' that will harness 'the transformative power of urbanisation'. Governments are enjoined to respond 'to this key development opportunity'. Any new urban model, they say, has 'to integrate all facets of sustainable development to promote equity, welfare and shared prosperity'. Above all, *'it's time to think urban'* (their emphasis).

These experts argue that 'a new urban governance must be based on aspirations for the right to the city, sustainable development and territorial equity'. They outline what needs to be achieved: 'strong multi-level governance frameworks, strengthening of decentralisation processes, promotion of integrated national urban and territorial policies, reinforcing metropolitan governance, promoting a new culture of participation and equity, strengthening capacity-building for urban governance, and enabling digital era governance'.[13] It's hard to disagree, given that nothing is left out.

The LSE's Urban Age programme has set the high bar in the enterprise of professional urban studies. It's mastered the art of talking Left while fundraising Right, saying a lot very persuasively whilst saying very little, sometimes saying nothing at all. It's a trendsetter and prototype for centres, initiatives and private-public urban partnerships around the globe.

Other professional projects now bankroll something called a 'new science of cities': ever more sophisticated modelling, Big Data, remote imaging of urban systems, image analysis, counting and classification, digital informational gathering, urban informatics, futuristic projections, and Smart Cities. This new science sees the city as a vast isotropic plane, as a seamless web of connectivity made up of the 'Internet of Things', an optimised city that factors out Jacobs's messiness. Instead we are promised a mesh of objects and entities interwoven in a smooth, frictionless space where people and information flow and business flourishes.

Smart Cities are seemingly the rage everywhere; both the public and private sector wrestle for a piece of this urban action. But what, exactly, is the action? Smart Cities are variously defined as 'Future Cities' and 'Intelligent Cities', cities that consummate the promise of digital technologies with their integration of 'multiple information and communication technology' (ICT). All of which will supposedly improve information systems in government, transportation, hospitals and schools, law enforcement and urban infrastructure. The British Standards Institute (BSI), 'a multinational business service provider', has set up a Smart Cities Framework Standard which, it claims, seeks 'to make excellence a habit'. The explicit focus is 'on enabling cities to: (a) make current and future citizen needs the driving force behind all city systems; (b) anticipate and respond to emerging challenges in a systematic, agile and sustainable way; and (c) create a step-change in the capacity for joined-up delivery and innovation across organisational boundaries within the city.'[14]

Like the language of this pronouncement, the future city is rendered banal, bereft of humanity. It has no lived-in streets, nothing warped, no snags or obstacles, no street vendors or people schmoozing, no intricate ballets or spontaneous improvisation, no Beats, no musty bookstores – only smart technology, algorithms and mathematical models. It's a future envisioned on the pattern of ordering stuff from Amazon. Each purchase we make there, each book-buying venture, enters into an algorithmic calculation based on a series of keywords. The next time we check out anything, we find a host of Amazon recommendations for future buys, oftentimes unnervingly accurate at identifying our tastes and even shaping new ones.

Imagine now something similar happening for a city. Every credit card transaction, every GPS usage, city street plan, subway and bus schedule, traffic flow pattern, planning authority hearings over, say, the past half-century, graphs of land and property prices, census tracts, housing tenures, electricity consumption, infrastructural maps – all this and a lot more could be fed into a model out of which algorithmic averages emerge, calculating our future 'optimal' city, how best it should be organised and governed. Such is the new science of the city, giving rise to new centres for its practice and implementation.

One is CUSP – Center for Urban Science Progress – based at New York University; corporate partners include Microsoft and Cisco Systems, with whom CUSP is out to brand its 'Urban Informatics'. 'New York City's government', CUSP confides in its promotional spiel, 'creates a terabyte of raw information every day about everything from parking tickets to electricity … Urban Informatics can give structure and new meaning to that set of data. … CUSP observes, analyses, and models cities to optimise outcomes, prototype new solutions, and formalise new tools and processes. At the same time, we engage students in the process, thus developing new expertise and experts in the field.'

This new science of the city is mesmerised by measurement and classification, by ranking and resilience. UN-Habitat recently announced it has devised a series of test scorecards in conjunction with IBM and the multinational engineering company AECOM, to develop a 'best practice against climate change'. A high score indicates that a city is 'future-proofed', which presumably means it has spent millions of dollars on the latest IBM and AECOM technology to get there.

Urban life is now reducible to endless indexes calculated by professional experts, consultants and tech companies: the most expensive city, the hippest, the happiest, the most habitable, the best to do business in, the most creative, eco-friendly, resilient, etc. These rosters reduce cities to essentially arbitrary sets of criteria that seem straight out of Borges and his essay on John Wilkins, like visiting some distant, invisible planet. How to quantify the impact of public space? How to measure what makes a city 'happy'? Can we really build a future reality by factoring out social reality?

Anybody who has ever read Baudelaire or Dostoevsky might query all this talk of happiness. Does a city exist to make people happy, anyway? A city can hardly be reduced to an algorithm, to a piece of pure data. Even when Amazon gets our book tastes right, it doesn't know why we like those books, why we read them, how we read them, how they inspire or energise us. So, too, with an urban algorithm. Can it really *get* what city life is about? No algorithm is ever likely to reproduce lines like these from Baudelaire:

> Swarming city, city gorged with dreams,
> Where ghosts by day pluck at the passersby,
> Everywhere mysteries flow like blood gushing,
> Through the narrow veins of a powerful colossus …

A real city isn't pure or full of 'haloes', as Baudelaire knew better than anyone. Baudelaire got down into the city's bowels, into its unconscious, to reach somewhere immeasurable, perhaps even unfathomable, venting his spleen along the way. He couldn't stomach anything 'pure', and wouldn't have stood for a lofty 'drinker of quintessences' or 'eater of ambrosia'. In one of his prose poems on Paris, 'Loss of Halo', a Baudelairean furtive describes the joy he feels at losing his halo one day, having it knocked off crossing the road and seeing it roll away into the dirt. He feels relief. Now, he can wander about incognito, commit vile deeds, abandon himself to debauchery – like 'ordinary mortals'. 'And so here I am', he says, no longer unimpeachable, 'only a man just like yourself.' And now some bad poet might pick the halo up, to the speaker's hilarity: 'Think of X! Think of Z! Oh! How amusing it will be!'

Baudelaire's contemporary, Dostoevsky, saw the city in much the same light – or, if you will, saw it shrouded in much the same shadow. For Dostoevsky, the city isn't about happiness but *intensity*. It's there to make us feel more alive, there not to flatten experience but to intensify it – to intensify authentic experience. Authentic experience is about *stimulation* rather than simulation, about free, unfettered expression and passionate self-development. Authentic experience doesn't come through the market. It isn't something you can buy, something derived from knowing all the answers, from sophisticated mathematical models. Instead, it comes from what Dostoevsky's Underground Man calls 'a craving for contrast and contradiction'.

The Underground Man speaks of his need for 'external sensations', his desire to plunge headlong into society, his 'anguished longing' to get out into the world. This is where the city comes into its own: cities externalise conflict and contradiction, contrast and stimulation. At least they ought to. This is a reality that can't be computed 'on the basis of any mathematical law', the Underground Man says, 'like a table of logarithms, and entered in an index'.

That's more a nightmare than a radiant dream, he says, because 'new economic relations will commence, ready-made and likewise calculated with mathematical precision, so that all possible answers will have been provided for them.' On the other hand, 'I wouldn't be surprised in the slightest if, suddenly, for no particular reason, in the midst of the universal future rational well-being, somebody … were to appear and, putting their hands on their hips, would say to us all: "How about it, why don't we knock this rational well-being into smithereens with one swift kick, with the sole purpose of sending all these logarithms to the devil!"'[15]

The Underground Man's 'craving for contrast and contradiction' places a special emphasis on the city street. There's a need to engage with the street, to sometimes stir oneself away from books, to enter into real life, to feel its thrills, its dangers and delights, its chaos and disorder. Phoney order bores the Underground Man, even disgusts him. One night, out on a roam, he glimpses a dance-floor brawl inside a tavern; a six-foot-plus army officer, brandishing billiard cues, is dispatching assailants out of the window. Enter the Underground Man, yearning to be thrown from the window himself! But, 'without a word of explanation', he's placed aside. The officer passes by 'as though he hadn't noticed me'. 'I could forgive blows,' he says, 'but I absolutely cannot forgive him for having moved me, for having completely failed to notice me.'

How to get even, how to make the officer take notice of him? How to make the world take notice of him? A duel? A literary quarrel? A missive in the mail? Quite by chance, the Underground Man spots his enemy one day strolling along Nevsky Prospect, St Petersburg's main boulevard, rarely moving aside for anybody, trampling imperviously through; this bully just walks over everybody, 'like they're empty space'. Ordinary people step aside, 'wriggle like eels', give way to him, to professional authority figures like him, those in power, those *with* power. It's a strange inflection of Jacobs's 'intricate sidewalk ballet'. But what if you don't give way? What if you stand your ground? Little by little, another idea takes hold.

At first, the Underground Man hesitates to stand his ground. In one attempt, at the last second, he loses his nerve and steps aside. Another time, ready to go for it, he stumbles and sprawls across the pavement, falling at the officer's feet. Afterwards, he's feverish for days. Then, unexpectedly, he sees his antagonist again one afternoon, out on Nevsky Prospect. This time, closing his eyes, he doesn't budge an inch, not one inch. 'He didn't even look round and pretended not to notice it', the Underground Man beams. 'But he was only pretending, I am convinced of that. I am convinced of that to this day! Of course, I got the worst of it – he was stronger, but that wasn't the point. The point was that I had attained my goal, that I had kept my dignity. I'd placed myself publicly on an equal social footing.'[16] And so, 'perhaps I am more alive than you are', the Underground Man taunts. 'Take a closer look at it! We don't even know where life lives now, or what it is, or what it's called ...'

We thus arrive at a theme that professional urbanists can't deal with very easily in their models: conflict and confrontation. The notion that cities are arenas for expressing conflict, for engaging in confrontation. Sometimes it's a confrontation with the self; other times it's confronting structures of social power. Usually, as with Dostoevsky's Underground Man, it's both, and usually at the same time. One of the enduring lessons Marxism has taught me over the years is how cities are spaces of collision, spaces of social struggle and class conflict. In other words, they're *political* realities; they can never be simply, or even complexly, paradigmatic – an algorithmic programme.

Cities are places where politics get worked through and worked out. They're places where contradictions get expressed, sometimes resolved; although resolutions are apt to lead to other sets of contradictions. Jane Jacobs knew about the intimacy of cities, about families and safety, hugs and kisses; yet, as an activist, she also knew how cities are equally defined by conflict and protest, by people demanding their rights, their right to the city. Cities push ordinary people around; but in cities ordinary people push back, assert themselves as individuals, affirm themselves as a public.

This has to be a crucial item in any amateur's arsenal: to be confrontational, to have a space to resist and oppose professional etiquette and ambition; to guard against professional domestication and being incorporated into the corporation. There's a long history of urban social movements, even of ordinary amateurs heading up cities themselves. According to Murray Bookchin (1921–2006), an anarchist scholar and activist who spent decades studying cities and their environments, past forms of urban governance were typically the domain of amateurs in defiance of professionals.

It wasn't professionals who ruled in these instances, but responsible citizens, starting with the *polis* of the ancient Greeks (where Pericles, Thucydides' 'first citizen of Athens', was an amateur), to the sixteenth-century Spanish Comuneros and eighteenth-century French Revolutionary communal councils, onwards on to pre-revolutionary New England town meetings and the 1871 Paris Commune councils, culminating with Spanish anarchists and the Popular Front collectives of 1936–37. In all these instances, Bookchin says, we glimpse the promise of 'a consciously amateur system of governance'. Paris, no less than Athens, was administered by amateurs – people who, for a few years and in their spare time, ran a city in revolutionary ferment.[17]

Amateurs awakened popular initiative, and imparted a sense of active purpose that no professional bureaucracy could hope to achieve, not then, perhaps not ever. Here the *polis* was governed by popular assemblies that met regularly, and the selection of 'civic officials' was carried out by sortition, or random lot, in the absence of top-down professionalism. Moreover, the *polis*, Bookchin says, 'wasn't only a treasured end in itself; it was the "school" in which the citizens' highest virtues were formed and found expression. Politics, in turn, wasn't only concerned with administering the affairs of the *polis* but with also educating the citizen as a public being who developed the competence to act in the public interest.'[18]

One of my own favourite urban movements with anarchist roots is the Situationists, a group of rebel artists, poets, filmmakers and political muckrakers who, during the 1950s and 1960s, epitomised confrontation and subversion. They never ran a city; but when they were active they made the city a lot more interesting and experimental, a lot more alive. Guy Debord belonged to the Situationists for a while. He was their urban strategist, their urban theorist, and Paris was his stomping ground and his laboratory.

In the 1950s, 'Paris was never asleep in its entirety,' Debord said, 'and permitted you to debauch and to change neighbourhoods three times each night. Its inhabitants hadn't yet been driven away and dispersed.' The city still had time for 'unmanageable riffraff', for 'the salt of the earth', for 'people quite sincerely ready to set the world on fire so that it had more brilliance'. In fact, the city was so beautiful then that many preferred to be poor there rather than rich elsewhere; they preferred, like Debord, to lead an 'openly independent life', finding themselves at home in 'the most ill-famed company'.[19]

What I still deeply admire about Guy Debord is his sense of provocation, his spirit of indignation, his desire to live a rich and full life, a poetic life – in spite of it all. 'I've seen only troubled times', Debord wrote at the beginning of *Panegyric*, his slim, elegant and elegiac autobiography; 'extreme divisions in society, and immense destruction; I have taken part in these troubles.' Debord was something of a prince of darkness, a prophet of storms: he lived through many, and conjured up a few more in his own imagination. 'Throughout the course of my adolescence', he said, 'I went slowly but inevitably towards a life of adventure, eyes open. I couldn't even think of studying for one of the learned professions that lead to holding down a job, for all of them seemed completely alien to my tastes and contrary to my opinions.'[20]

The people Debord most esteemed in the world were two poets of absolute irreverence and scandal, Arthur Cravan and Isidore Ducasse, alias Comte de Lautréamont, both of whom died mysteriously and at tender ages. In Lautréamont, Debord saluted the true inventor of *détournement* – literally a 'rerouting' or 'hijacking' – a favoured pastime of the Situationists, who practiced as well as preached *détournement*. They hijacked and rerouted all things, all 'professional' things, from the art market to the literature industry, from parliamentary politics to the ideology of urbanism.

A prime example was the Dutch Situationist artist Constant Nieuwenhuys's prototypical city, 'New Babylon', which rerouted the Protestant association of Babylon with evil and sex: 'Babylon the great, mother of whores and of earth's abominations', said the Book of Revelation (17:5). For Constant and Debord, the accursed city of Satan, the great whore Babylon – where a fear of fornication and impurity becomes bound up with a fear of the city – symbolised the good city of the future. Debord coined the name one winter's night back in 1959, when he'd enthusiastically greeted Constant's preliminary drawing-board visions. Constant was taken by the idea of 'Dériville', until Debord proposed 'New Babylon'.

In New Babylon, Constant modelled *dérive,* something Debord had defined as 'a mode of experimental behaviour linked to the conditions of urban society: a technique of rapid passage through varied ambiances'. New Babylon sought to expose the ruse of professional urbanism, *détourning* it for the sake of disalienation: 'We need to defend ourselves at all times from the bards of conditioning – and reverse their rhythms.' Constant dreamed of redolent passageways, shocking landscapes, a holistic urban environment that brimmed with texture, tone, and topographic fantasy. His designs superimposed routes and spaces on other routes and spaces, sometimes on old cityscapes, other times on completely new neighbourhoods. Some visions are exhilarating, brightly coloured, deconstructed landscapes, plexiglass models of futuristic cities; elsewhere they resemble sublime Piranesian labyrinths, an Eternal City of romance and ruin.

Throughout the 1950s and '60s, Debord and his Situationist crew – he likened them to 'demolition experts' – inhabited their own little Piranesian patch of Paris, each side of the Seine, their own 'zone of perdition' where, Debord said, his 'youth went as if to achieve its education'.[21] Yet by the mid-1970s this pungent, shady underworld of fantastical adventure and urban possibility was well-nigh gone, assassinated in the name of capitalist economic progress and sound planning, with the blessing of career politicians. *The Assassination of Paris* was the title of Louis Chevalier's damning 1977 autopsy on Gallic urbicide, which denounced those 'polytechnicians' – the elite civil servants trained at France's *grandes écoles* – who had systematically orchestrated the deadly *coup de grâce.*

Chevalier took his native city to heart, agonised over its woes – 'With Les Halles gone, Paris is gone' – and Debord acknowledged an affinity. 'It could almost be believed, despite the innumerable earlier testimonies of history and the arts, that I was the only person to have loved Paris; because, first of all, I saw no one else react to this question in the repugnant "seventies". But subsequently I learned that Louis Chevalier, its old historian, had published then, without too much being said about it, *The Assassination of Paris*. So we could count at least two righteous people in the city at that time.'[22]

Debord was fascinated by the low city, by an urbanism that was musty and worn, by a city both bawdy and beautiful, without haloes, the sort of urban paradise that Baudelaire evoked in *Le Voyage*: 'To plunge into the abyss ... And find in the depths of the unknown the new'. Debord's city is one predicated on a 'unitary urbanism'; physical and social sundering are here stitched back together. But unity doesn't express uniformity; instead, it implies chance and uncertainty, insubordination rather than docility, a love of the past combined with a yearning for the future, for things not yet seen, for a reality yet to be.

'Our epoch accumulates power and imagines itself rational', says a voiceover in another of Debord's experimental films, *Critique of Separation*, from 1961. 'Yet no one recognises these powers as their own. Nowhere is there entry into adulthood, only the transformation one day of this long anxiety into a measured sleep. The question isn't that people live more or less poorly but always that the rules of their life escape them.' Then a subtitle flashes up, urging another intent: 'To give each person the social space essential for the full expression of life'.

5

Work in the Crystal Palace

The Organisation for Economic Cooperation and Development (OECD) reports that a third of the world's population, almost two billion souls, now engage in irregular occupations, undocumented and self-reliant. These activities generate a staggering net worth of $10 trillion, earnings bettered only by the US economy ($14 trillion). As productivity grows in the global economy, its 'official' rank-and-file workforce shrinks, and a quasi-spontaneous system of self-employment prevails, a cutting and pasting of economic life. Its self-generating rate of job creation puts any government to shame: no Walmart or Microsoft, no multinational or supra-international can compete, no private or public institution. By 2020, the OECD reckons that two-thirds of the workers of the world will have no workplace to go to. They'll be engaged in some form of informality, a system now often generically known as '*Système D*'.

'*Système D*' is the slang term used in the French Caribbean and Africa for *débrouillards* (from *se débrouiller*: to sort oneself out, to get by unaided), those resourceful pedlars and hustlers, hawkers and street vendors who scavenge their way through life, who deploy their will and their wits at street markets and unlicensed bazaars around the globe. Here self-reliance means self-reproduction, a form of autonomous survival, although, for others, it also means 'defiance'. 'System D' has come to replace what everybody used to call the 'informal' sector, with its connotations of clandestinity, of shady wheeling and dealing, a criminal underworld off the map of 'respectable' economic gain. But as journalist Robert Neuwirth suggests, it's a mistake to see this system as 'a kind of bastard ward of the state – a zone that is kept around because it ensures that people will have the minimum income required to survive, and thus will not revolt against the existing order'.[1]

In fact, System D is now so globally widespread, Neuwirth says, so crucial as an earner for *all* nations, so tied to the 'formal sector', that it's a respectable and honest form of employment, a giant economy populated by workers regardless of specific nationality, 'strikingly independent, yet deeply enmeshed in the legal world'. 'It involves small-scale entrepreneurs but links them to global trading circuits. It's the economic way of the global majority, guided not by corporations or politicians or economists, but by ordinary citizens.'

Neuwirth says that 'economic refugees' help swell the ranks of System D. Importantly, though, he's not talking about foreigners or overseas immigrants here so much as people displaced from the regular workplace, the men and women pushed out of steady economic life, especially after the financial crisis of 2008; and not only factory and industrial labourers, but every category of worker – white-collar, blue-collar and no-collar – in the developed as well as developing countries.

In the US, a recent census estimates that 27 million Americans – around one-fifth of the overall workforce – work part-time; 9 million of them admit they've been forced into part-time work because they couldn't find a full-time job. Meanwhile, around 3.4 million others classify themselves as independent, working full-time (and sometimes more than full-time), yet are wholly on their own, self-employed, bearing the costs of health insurance and pension contributions out of their own pockets. There are many others who work extra jobs, second and sometimes third jobs, for hourly wages, at piecemeal rates, with zero-hours contracts, without any benefits or security, without rights.

This, of course, is the fitful reality of the 'precariate', those insecure workers who earn their keep in the ever-expanding 'gig' economy, perhaps the most dynamic sector of our urbanising economy. Temps and freelancers, contractors and start-up entrepreneurs, decoupled from the workplace, frequently decoupled from anyplace, now define the future of work pretty much everywhere. By 2020, estimates suggest that 40 per cent of American workers will be independents. They're a Millennial generation workforce with little prospect – whether they want it or not – of ever having a steady job with anything conceivably described as a 'career path'.

Employment here will be the jobs that people invent themselves, with their own computers, sitting in their own homes, or in some Starbucks nearby. The Freelance Union, a US group, estimates that 53 million Americans currently freelance their living, a figure set to rise dramatically over the next decade.[2] According to Britain's Office for National Statistics, by the beginning of 2017 the nation's self-employed workforce will exceed numbers employed in the public sector. Self-employment now accounts for 4.76 million workers in the UK, of which 2 million form the 'knowledge economy'; public sector staff has shrunk to 5.33 million people and will continue its downward trend. Once upon a time, workers in Britain belonged to either the private or public sector, with little alternative; now they slip somewhere between sectors, straddle a dialectic between self-empowerment and self-enslavement.

Secure employment contracts accrue only to a privileged minority. 'The new world of work', the *Financial Times* said in 2015, 'must chart a course between the twin dangers of corporate conformism and worker exploitation'. These twin dangers loom large over today's professionalised labour market, impacting on the labour process, defining its prospects and possibilities, its anxieties and algorithms.

For these 'privileged' professionals, conformism plays out as a desperate need to defend your contingent benefits, to cling onto them, to do anything that ensures your employability, your *indispensability*. In consequence, professional employees aren't usually forced into working hard: they cajole themselves into it, they never stop working. They perform voluntarily, tailor their whole personalities to the job, *become* the job, weld professional work and personal life into one seamless unholy alliance.

The professional workplace has changed a lot over the past half-century. In the late 1950s, the American novelist and satirist Alan Harrington wrote a quirky non-fiction account of *Life in the Crystal Palace*, centring around his many years working in public relations for an unnamed US corporation (actually, Standard Oil, in New Jersey).[3] One-time pal of Jack Kerouac and Allen Ginsberg, Harrington was a chip off Dostoevsky's block, typically mixing black humour with poetic imagination, mockery (and frequently self-mockery) with biting social critique. As *Life in the Crystal Palace* suggests, Dostoevsky's spirit haunts Harrington's stint at the corporation. Having a steady job, being a company man, wearing a neutral grey suit, having a pension, a chance to enjoy an entire lifetime anxiety-free as an employee, amiable, decent, polite, co-operative, unsackable – what could be better?

And the Crystal Palace, that glimmering symbol of corporate professional life, is nothing less than the headquarters of the Good Society, of the happy life. Here all frustrations are banished. 'We're not worried about our jobs, about the future, about much of anything.' 'Even in younger men', Harrington says, 'the hard muscle of ambition tends to go slack after a while. Gradually you become accustomed to the Utopian drift. When we moved to the suburbs, the company paid its employees' moving expenses and helped them settle in their new homes.' After a while, Harrington

began to feel what I now recognise was a gradually deepening contentment. If you are on the watch for symptoms, here are a few: (1) You find that you are planning your life defensively, in terms of savings plans and pensions, rather than thinking speculatively. (2) You become much less impatient over inefficiency, shrug your shoulders and accept it as the way things are. (3) Your critical faculties become dull; you accept second-best; it seems unsporting to complain. (4) Nothing makes you nervous. (5) You find that you are content to talk to people without saying anything. (6) You mention something like 'our Human Development Department' to outsiders and learn with surprise that they think you made a joke.

'I can't even get sick anymore', says Harrington. 'This will sound ridiculous, but when the company obtained a supply of influenza shots, I found myself in the absurd position of refusing one. For some reason I wanted a chance to resist the flu in my own way.'

Eventually Harrington is overcome by 'a feeling of being in limbo'. 'More than ever', he says, 'one feels – ungratefully –

over-protected. While on the job, I actually can't feel hot or cold.' 'What's the moral of all this?' Harrington asks. 'I'm not quite sure, but some time ago Dostoevsky put it in *Notes from Underground*: "In the Crystal Palace suffering is unthinkable. You believe, do you not, in a Crystal Palace which shall be forever unbreakable – in an edifice, that is to say, at which no one shall be able to put out his tongue, or in any other way to mock? ... I should fight shy of such a building."'

Underground Man Harrington could never accept the numbing security of 1950s corporate America. At heart, he's a confrontational personality, an amateur fighting shy of professionalism, an amateur fighting shy of the Crystal Palace, standing up against the monotony of cubicle life, sticking his tongue out – just to live a bit, just to feel more alive.

But, circa 2016, it's a curious thing reading Harrington's tale of middle-brow corporate life, his parable of pre-Reaganite working America. Indeed, to believe this world still bases itself on a comfy career for life, and that contentedness and rationality prevail, is an absurdity, a cruel joke. How different things have become! If we want to see a real incarnation of Dostoevsky's Crystal Palace in our third-millennium professionalised future, we should look no further than Dave Eggers's novel *The Circle*, his barely fictionalised parable of the corporation the Circle, an omnipotent, multi-grained, decaffeinated dream conglomerate modelled on Google, Microsoft and Facebook, set in a dazzling Californian campus, 'wild with Pacific colour'.

Here the Harrington utopia of a job for life has transformed into a dystopic job to the death, a death in paradise, where once-flabby contentment has given way to lean, jittery anxiety; life in work means having no life, existing in permanent fear of being *dispensable*, of performing less well than your peers. Nothing is hidden anymore; all is transparent and trackable, observable and quantifiable. Nobody *doesn't* participate in this system. As somebody reminds Eggers's protagonist Mae Holland, the young woman who's recruited wholesale into the Circle's professionalised ideal: 'Don't you see, Mae, that it's all connected? You play your part. You have to *part*-icipate.' At the Circle, your participation rank is common knowledge. 'We see this workplace as a community,' another colleague tells Mae, 'and every person who works here is part of that community.'[4]

Gone is the dreary, fluorescent working environment, the rationally arranged Taylorist rows of desks familiar to Harrington. In the 1910s, Frederick W. Taylor had defined 'scientific' principles of workplace management, based on efficiency drives and highly detailed divisions of labour; no time was wasted, all the hours of the working day were filled with activity, a non-stop chain of routines. This paradigm dominated factory and office working life in the post-war era, and was responsible for much of the alienation of 'modern times'.

Yet, a half-century on, designed workspaces, sometimes by signature architects, are conceived for ultimate seduction and persuasion. Alienation these days seems much less alienating. Honeycomb-like, with bright primary-coloured partitions and soft-toned lighting, desk zones now get punctuated by ping-pong tables and espresso machines, relieved by gyms and swimming pools, napping niches and bonsai trees, all gently coaxing workers to be more and more active and motivated. Design is there to entice commitment and to extract effort.[5]

It's another way to make workers *happy*. One of the US's real-life workplace gurus, Tony Hsieh, CEO of Zappos, argues that most successful businesses are those that 'deliberately and strategically nurture happiness throughout their organisations'. Zappos is renowned for redefining the convivial workplace, for being attentive to bottom-line dictates while nurturing committed and contented employees. (Staff are encouraged to bring their dogs to work.) The company is proud of its tag line: 'Deliver WOW!' Its online clothing and shoe business now has annual revenues of over $2 billion. Headquartered in Las Vegas, Zappos is a wholly owned subsidiary of Amazon (snapped up for $1.2 billion in 2009), with around 1,500 employees, where 'chief happiness officers ensure that nobody escapes workplace happiness.'[6] Hsieh suggests that corporate bosses across America should follow suit. First they should sack the most downbeat 10 per cent of their employees; afterwards, the remainder will become 'super-engaged'.

Over the past year or so, Hsieh has introduced a new management style at Zappos, something called 'Holacracy', a boss-free workplace philosophy that vividly brings to real life the ideals of Eggers's Circle. Under Holacracy, all authority is distributed and diffused, and employees are empowered in a 'new peer-to-peer operating system that increases transparency, accountability, and organisational agility'.

'Research shows', Hsieh said, explaining Holacracy, 'that every time the size of a city doubles, innovation and productivity per resident increases by 15 per cent. But when companies get bigger, innovation or productivity per employee generally goes down. So we're trying to figure out how to structure Zappos more like a city, and less like a bureaucratic corporation. In a city, people and businesses are self-organising. We're trying to do the same thing by switching from a normal hierarchical structure to a system called Holacracy, which enables employees to act more like entrepreneurs and self-direct their work instead of reporting to a manager who tells them what to do.'

Yet in April 2016, a *New York Times* blog reported a strange occurrence: 'The Zappos Exodus Continues'. The corporate mouthpiece, *Forbes* magazine, soon followed up with a more detailed article, wondering 'What's Causing Zappos to "Hemorrhage" Talent?' Both publications revealed 'the sad tale of Zappos', 'long known as a great place to work'. The problem was that since the previous March, Zappos had lost 260 employees, about 18 per cent of its once-happy workforce, who had suddenly got unhappy and walked out the door. What went wrong?

Holacracy, apparently. 'Zappos now risks killing the goose that laid golden eggs for its customers and parent corporation Amazon for years. You can't make a workplace better by shoving an executive team's favourite version of self-directed leadership down its employees' throats.'[7] 'It's beyond ironic', *Forbes* magazine continues, 'that Zappos wants its employees to get excited about losing hierarchy in the operation when the hierarchical structure is exactly what allowed the leadership to force "Holacracy" into place.' 'Anyone who didn't accept Holacracy', Hseih is quoted as saying, 'could take a generous buyout.' Still, the message of Zappos rings out clearly: 'Get in line or get out!'

No matter how seductive and 'happy' the workplace, it seems you can't escape the reality that employees are human widgets used and discarded at the behest of bosses. All that really counts for a firm is your VORP – 'Value Over a Replacement Player'. It's a brutal realist notion that takes no prisoners. You're indispensable so long as there's nobody else around who can perform better, who's more skilful, more self-reliant and compliant, and ready to work even harder than you. 'Companies burn you out and churn you out when somebody better, or cheaper, becomes available.'[8] Although you don't get fired anymore: you 'graduate' from the workplace, the new euphemism in business babble. Your cheery ex-boss is delighted for you, hosting a farewell party, excited to see how you will use your superpowers in your next big work adventure.

At HubSpot, another high-tech start-up, founded in Cambridge, Massachusetts in 2006, there's a similar slick and happy veneer, 'with beanbag chairs and unlimited vacation – a corporate utopia where there's no need for work-life balance because work is life and life is work. Imagine a frat house mixed with a kindergarten mixed with Scientology, and you have an idea of what it's like.'[9] But despite the cool office interior there's no job security. It's a digital sweatshop where young people, packed side by side at long tables, hunched over laptops rather than sewing machines, stare into their screens for hours on end, barking commands into headsets, trying to sell software, selling themselves in the process. 'The free snacks are nice,' is what one ex-employee said, 'but you must tolerate having your head stuffed with silly jargon and ideology about being on a mission to change the world … Wealth is generated, but most of the loot goes to a handful of people at the top, the founders and venture capital investors.'

This kind of manufactured happiness gets under your skin. William Davies calls it the 'Happiness Industry', which valorises your emotions, our emotions, converting them into smiling surplus value. Happiness gets under your skin at Dave Eggers's Circle, just like at Zappos or HubSpot. You become the company, you sleep it, eat it, procreate it. Is this real happiness? Perhaps Harrington's peers really were happy? But here, at the Circle, it's no longer a happy suburban *Leave It to Beaver* so much as a menacing *Day of the Locust*; and the locusts are now inside you, inside your head, eating away. Mae Holland is smitten and bitten, seemingly happy and content, and at times she sounds a lot like Chernyshevsky's heroine Vera Pavlovna from *What Is to Be Done?* only in wide-awake not dream time:

A few thousand Circlers began to gather in the twilight, and standing among them, Mae knew that she never wanted to work – never wanted to be – anywhere else. Her hometown, and the rest of California, the rest of America, seemed like some chaotic mess in the developing world. Outside the walls of the Circle, all was noise and struggle, failure and filth. But here, all had been perfected.

The Circle even has an Underground Man – a guy called Mercer, Mae's ex-boyfriend, a loser because he doesn't want in, because he knows it's a scam: he's there to stick his tongue out at the Crystal Palace. Mae once loved him but now hates his guts. He's her past, the mess outside, antiquarian bullshit; he spends his time on his passion, making chandeliers out of dead animal parts. 'Here's the thing,' Mercer tells Mae in one fraught scene,

'and it's painful to say this to you. But you're not very interesting anymore. You sit at a desk twelve hours a day and you have nothing to show for it except for some numbers that won't exist or be remembered in a week. You're leaving no evidence that you lived. There's no proof.'

'Fuck you, Mercer.'

'And worse, you're not *doing* anything interesting anymore. You're not seeing anything, saying anything. The weird paradox is that you think you're at the center of things, and that makes your opinions more valuable, but you yourself are becoming less vibrant. I bet you haven't done anything offscreen in months. Have you?'

'You're such a fucker, Mercer.'

But Mercer's big problem is wanting out. Somehow, he's worse being offline than on, worse unplugging himself and fleeing than standing his ground and engaging. It's like sheltering under a tree during a lightning strike. He writes Mae one last note:

> By the time you read this, I'll be off the grid, and I expect that others will join me. In fact, I *know* others will join me. We'll be living underground, and in the desert, in the woods. We'll be like refugees, or hermits, some unfortunate but necessary combination of the two. Because this is what we are. I expect this is some second great schism, where two humanities will live, apart but parallel. There will be those who live under the surveillance dome you're helping to create, and those who live, or try to live, apart from it. I'm scared to death for us all.

Mercer is right to be scared: while fleeing in his pickup truck, SeeChange cameras track him and drones hunt him down. In fierce determination to get out, to escape beyond their gaze, Mercer ploughs his vehicle through a barrier and careens into a gorge – death is the only escape. It's all on film, recorded, remarked upon: 'Mae, you were trying to help a very disturbed, antisocial young man. You and the other participants were reaching out, trying to bring him into the embrace of humanity, and he rejected that.'

There's actually another Underground Man in Eggers's Crystal Palace. In many ways, this character is more politically satisfying than Mercer, more of a dialectical personality. He's an amateur masquerading as a pro, an insider who's also an outsider. Wearing 'an enormous hoodie', he even looks like a contemporary Underground Man, an Occupier or black bloc rebel. This Underground Man is none other than the Circle's boy-wonder visionary, Tyler

Gospodinov, the company's first 'Wise Man', whom everybody knows as Ty. Mae knows him as Kalden, Ty's amateur alter ego, his shadow self: a kind of Edward Snowden whistle-blower who warns of the closing of the Circle, the fulfilment of the totalitarian nightmare he's helped to create. The closing of the Circle means that the professional world will be finally and forever sealed off from what lies beyond it, outside its boundaries. Outside is the chaotic mess that Mae recoils from, what remains, if anything does, of our non-corporate public life. Out there, there's filth and failure, noise and struggle. Inside the Circle, the TruYou prevails: 'One button for the rest of your life online.'

Kalden isn't running away from this inside – he's hacking it, trying to disassemble it from within. But he needs help; he reaches out to Mae, seeing her as ambivalent, as still a potential subverter, a twisted dialectician who still has amateurism in her blood. But as events progress, she's too far gone already. Too straight, too professionally assimilated, too corporately acculturated. The other Wise Men, says Kalden, have 'professionalised our idealism, monetarised our utopia'. They 'saw the connection between our work and politics, and between politics and control. Public-private leads to private-private, and soon you have the Circle running most or even all government services, with incredible private-sector efficiency and an insatiable appetite.' It's an ominous prediction.

Kalden knows more than Mercer. He's an outsider-insider, a maggot in the apple, attempting to eat his way out from the core. He's not so much a refuser as a double agent, calling out to others, to fellow underground men and women who aren't unplugged and offline but tuned in, masters and mistresses of both worlds, who understand the limitations of each. Because they know the score, they know how to strategise and how to disrupt. Their value systems are still intact – authentic, we might say. All of these people know how resistance these days isn't so much about what you do as who you *are*: it's ontological more than epistemological, something that cuts right inside you, into your beliefs, into your democratic hopes, into your anti-corporate desires. Resistance, in other words, needs to be wholesale, a total way of being. 'There used to be the option of opting out', Kalden says at the end of *The Circle*. 'But now that's over. ... The Circle needs to be dismantled.'

Over the years, I've found myself being both a Mercer and a Kalden, an outsider as well as an insider, an Underground Man as well as an overground man. The two impulses have tugged away inside me. Conceptually, in my head, I know that the inside is the place to do good work, to earn a living, to stand up for your principles, to have a platform for affirming those principles. And, as an insider, people usually listen to you. But, instinctively and impulsively, impetuously, I know that the inside is corrupt and co-opting. So the underground grips me: I want to walk away, run away like Mercer, watch from the outside as the whole inside blows up, like V dynamiting London's Old Bailey in *V for Vendetta*, amid a rollicking Tchaikovskian fanfare.

I'm fortunate here. Or unfortunate, depending on how you see it: I found my passion in life. It helped me escape, into the wilderness. It's been a blessing and a curse, certainly a challenge. For there's no career in my passion, never will be. That makes life hard, because there are few job openings. But I got my chance, a second chance actually, and took it, coming across this passion in a strange place: *books*. I'm still not sure whether certain books led me to being a contrarian or being a contrarian led me to certain books, like *Notes from Underground*. But books helped me articulate the politics inside me, which dumbfounded me, which yearned to break out of me. Books explained why I'd felt adrift in and between those tiresome, ridiculous jobs I'd once had. Books planted seeds in my head, flowering into a realisation: that I could never fit into any professionalised world.

I might not be the only one. These days, corporations preach the virtues of inclusion and participation at work, of Holacracy and the like, sometimes hiring expensive 'motivational consultants' to get staff enthused and psyched up. Yet the more money bosses throw at boosting productivity, at attempting to inspire staff enthusiasm and commitment, the more sluggish and indifferent many of these employees become. Big-time slackers get fired, as Tony Hsieh suggested they should, replaced by eager debutantes, by more mal-leable human material. But after a while, even they begin to flag.

The reason is perhaps obvious: the senselessness of the work involved, its meaningless nature, makes it impossible to feel moti-vated, to feel personally connected to what you do for the bulk of your waking hours. It's a terrible waste of people's potential, a veritable human tragedy. Sluggishness equates to apathy, which in turn prompts more sluggishness. No carrot and stick can ever animate deadened bodies and deadened minds, deadened souls.

Every year in Europe, Repetitive Strain Injury (RSI) increases by 20 per cent. In the paper-pushing, keyboard-tapping and check-out-scanning service sector, RSI rises as much as 50 per cent each year. The French National Agency for the Improvement of Work Conditions (ANACT) suggests that musculoskeletal disorder is 'an illness resulting from actions that are deprived of meaning'. Gallup polls show how only around 13 per cent of the global workforce might be described as 'actively engaged'. On the other hand, in the US and Europe, some 20 per cent of employees are 'actively disengaged'.[10]

Disengagement costs the capitalist economy dearly, as much as $550 billion each year. Importantly, we're not talking about mass walkouts and general strikes here; it's more a problem of absenteeism, due to sickness and fatigue and burn-out. Meanwhile, other more diffuse forms of struggle gnaw away inside the system. They're seldom channelled explicitly through a union, via old-fashioned collective bargaining. Instead, resistance is often more a matter of dragging one's feet, of absenteeism and slowdowns. It's about being counter-productive, about draining the system of its legitimacy, about being unwilling to equate one's life with the inexorable flow of useless commodities – which takes away the necessity of having to work to afford them.

The dab hand of 'anti-economics', Guillaume Paoli, has taken this state of affairs to task; he's put his own existential gloss on Marx's famous falling rate of profit thesis. Paoli argues that in the modern workplace there's a concurrent tendency for the *rate of motivation to plummet as well*. In fact, at the very moment when global capital seems to have reached its ultimate exterior constraining limits, an internal factor threatens: the growing dissatisfaction of human resources, without which capital is nothing. The limits to capital, then, aren't technological but *subjective*: subjectivity is the political fault line of the future.[11]

Thus, when a professional ruling class appeals to everybody to lean in, to get motivated, to thrive together, a crisis of motivation deepens. It's a negative correlation, unavoidably – and a good thing too. 'Do I really want to live this way?' Paoli asks. 'What am I willing to sacrifice for it?' He asks whether the task for the radical Left is to invoke full employment, striving for an economy with more low-end, pointless and meaningless jobs (jobs usually short on pay as well as sense), or to politically harness demotivation, to leverage it strategically so as to bring the workplace down: to hack it because we are hacked off. This would be a radically different 'right to laziness', a different slant to participation.

What appears passive and resigned is actually active and some-times surprisingly upbeat – only it doesn't seem so. People aren't so much duped as silently conscious dissenters in the popular ranks. We might say they're what Guillaume Paoli implies: they're the offspring of Bartleby, the hero of Herman Melville's 1855 novella about an odd scrivener. They're people who 'would prefer not to', who vote with their feet by not voting; they desist from doing their allotted work because they prefer not to, because they would prefer to be doing something else. As Melville writes: 'Nothing so aggravates an earnest person as a passive resistance.' 'There was something about Bartleby', admits the narrator, his 'austere reserve', 'his gentle tone', something 'that not only strangely disarmed me, but, in a wonderful manner, touched and disconcerted me'. 'Why do you refuse?' Bartleby's boss asks, why refuse to examine a small bit of paper? 'I would prefer not to', says Bartleby. 'At present I would prefer not to be a little reasonable.'[12]

In the mid-1990s, Guillaume Paoli helped establish a radical collective across Germany and France called *Les Chômeurs Heureux*, or 'The Happy Unemployed', taking up Bartleby's challenge in brilliantly innovative ways. They deployed a won-derful *détournement*, a wonderful rerouting of that most radical poet of negation: Comte de Lautréamont, infamous author of Surrealist classics *Les Chants de Maldoror* and *Poésies*. In *Poésies*, from 1870, Lautréamont wrote: 'Up to now, misfortune has been described in order to inspire terror and pity. I will describe hap-piness, in order to inspire the contrary.'[13] This was the radical cue for the Happy Unemployed: all that has hitherto been taken as misfortune, inspiring terror and pity, like unemployment, is now good fortune, something inspiring the very opposite, which is to say, joy and affirmation.

Many people, from the far Right to the far Left, are always up in arms about unemployment, always struggling *against* it, the Happy Unemployed say; always trying to dam its torrential flow. Yet the effort is futile. Many see unemployment as a dirty word, as a negative label, a pathology. To be unemployed is to be a worker without work. But must we forever define ourselves by work, as workers, and nothing else? Because everyone knows, even if they know very little, that unemployment will never be eradicated from our society, such as it is organised and run: 'The factory's going badly? You lay off workers. The factory's going well? You invest in new automation and lay off workers.'[14] It's a no-win situation – no-win for everybody except professional bosses and owners.

But what if you imagine something else; what if the reaction was, 'I've just been laid off: great!' A small group of unemployed people, along with Paoli, started to imagine this scenario and promulgate its implications to a wider public. In 1995, they published their *Manifesto of the Happy Unemployed* (updating it in 2006 and 2013). Quickly, maybe more quickly than they ever thought, the collective grabbed a lot of mostly incredulous media attention, getting talked about in the press and making guest appearances on German and French TV. They started to organise public events, low-key street events where happy unemployed people could encounter other unemployed people, and perhaps not-so-happy employed people as well.

In the centre of Hamburg, in early 2000, they rolled out not the red carpet but the green baize, transforming a dreary pedestrian shopping street into a verdant lawn, setting out chaises longues and trestle tables. People were encouraged to linger, to man the barbecue, to drink beer, and hear about unemployment and how to resolve it. It was rare for anybody to act aggressively. The overwhelming sentiment was one of sympathy and understanding – more understanding than the mainstream media displayed.

The point of these initiatives was to get people to stop, forget about what they were doing and engage in festival, in celebration, creating a sort of agora in which people could enjoy the principal advantage of being jobless: the blessing of TIME. We have nothing of our own but time; you don't live twice, neither as amateurs nor professionals; time waits for no one. So why waste it in senseless work? Public events like the one in Hamburg were a kind of 'Jobless Pride', where hitherto invisible and isolated people without jobs became visible again, met other people without jobs, and formed a conscious collective with time on its hands, discussing political affairs in public.

Many unemployed people are glad they no longer live on the rack. But the perpetual menace is bureaucratic harassment and humiliation, the constant professional intrusion into their private lives. You have to prove you're 'actively seeking work', actively seeking pointless work that nobody needs, that nobody would ever miss, that lasts too long and pays too little. The image of the Happy Unemployed is thus an ideal type, or archetype, permitting the question to be posed about the obstacles to its own realisation. Exposed here is the absurdity that conditions the labour market, an absurdity like all other market absurdities.

If the jobless person is 'unhappy', it isn't usually because they can't find work: it's because they don't have any money. 'We say don't demand work, demand money; not actively seeking work but actively seeking money.' Or, as the Happy Unemployed put it, in an intriguing phrase: 'actively seeking obscure resources'.[15] Part of those obscure resources has been commandeered by the professional managerial class whose members patrol and survey the world of employment and unemployment; who doctor the job figures, hawk banalities about job creation and workfare, man the dole centres and government agencies, and frequently pay themselves too much.

Imagine, then, how such obscure resources might become less obscure and more available: eliminate control measures against the unemployed, shut down all those agencies that manipulate statistics and keep tabs, and lay off those professional managers. This wouldn't be a bad contribution to budget restrictions and austerity drives; afterwards, the sums saved might be redirected to automatic and unconditional allocations to the unemployed – ex-professionals included.

Meantime, if the jobless are unhappy, it's also because work is over-hyped as a value. As though its opposite – unemployment – meant boredom, nothing to do, not knowing anybody, social exclusion.

But can we take advantage of being beings with that inestimable existential resource? Time would be time for amateurism, time for meaningful 'specialisation', time for finding your passion, your true calling. The roster of listless, reluctant, bored professionals – even highly paid professionals – is long, and I bet growing as we speak. They're performing as themselves despite themselves. Do people really dream of being corporate lawyers or merchant bankers, private equity managers and tax accountants? Do these people still dream? Aren't we such stuff as dreams are made on?

One great romantic dream is to imagine a society that breaks free of the vicious circle of undefined productivity, of productivity for productivity's sake, of accumulation for the sake of capital accumulation. Marx wrote *Capital* as a manifesto on how capitalism generalises unemployment; he warned of the progressive production of a 'relative surplus population' whose destiny is entirely contingent on the whims of the business cycle. Yet, at the same time, Marx also worked away at his *Grundrisse* manuscript, his own more exploratory 'notebooks' that were never destined to be published. (They never were in his lifetime.) There, he penned passages with bold leaps of the utopian imagination. Even in this dire system, Marx thought, immanent possibilities reside for a planet that's been urbanised and transformed into a vast arena of 'fixed capital'.

More than a century-and-a-half on, Marx's reality is the here and now: the only labour that really seems to count today isn't the labour of hardware but the labour of thoughtware – immaterial labour, cognitive no-collar capitalism. Marx's tack in the *Grundrisse* is that of an optimist: he sees a world that 'suspends living labour' to revolve around 'dead labour', that produces social life under the domain of the 'general intellect', that organises production around automation and high technology, is a society equipped with all the powers to reduce 'necessary labour' time. All the instruments are available, all the wherewithal is here, he says, for creating socially disposable time, for reducing labour time to a bare minimum. Everyone's time could be freed up to let them engage in a more passionate and fulfilling life *after* work.

But this vision of a post-work future is a future denied, stymied by the ideology of employment for employment's sake and the dogma of productivity, perpetuated and promulgated by a professional ruling class that cajoles and seduces us into accepting its productivist meme as a given, as the only possible reality. Work is good, therefore we must work. These professionals have parasitised our minds. It's they who adjudicate worthiness and rank; it's they who forever tut-tut those without work.

What counts isn't the effort or the pleasure that flows from that effort, but the enslavement of labour to capital. What counts isn't the satisfaction that flows from the act of labour, but the status of the social relationship that commands production. Effort isn't productive unless it's made at the behest of some professional. Economists can't deal with the notion of human validity outside of the corporation, outside of stock value, outside of shareholder dividend, outside of cost-benefit, outside of a market.

Work for most people means time spent doing something that has absolutely no meaning for the doer. It is an alienated activity, with an alienated product (if there is a product), commandeered by an alienating organisation, all conspiring to shape an alienated self. Many twenty- and thirty-somethings these days are learning how to re-evaluate their 'career' choices, as well as the whole notion of career itself, because they're smart enough to know that they might not have anything deemed a 'career' anymore. In fact, there's an entire cohort of college-educated young people who recognise they'll never work a 'proper' salaried job. They're not turned on by temping or interning, either, not interested in the 'gig' economy.

Perhaps, during crises, during the crisis we seem permanently to inhabit today, we can plot alternative survival programmes, methods enabling us not so much to 'earn a living' as 'live a living'. Perhaps we can self-downsize and address the torment of work that forever haunts: work is revered in our culture, yet at the same time workers are becoming superfluous; you loathe your job, your boss, the servility of what you do and how you do it, the pettiness of the tasks involved, yet you want to keep your job at all costs. You see no way of defining yourself other than through work. Perhaps there's a point at which we can all be pushed over the edge, like the Underground Man, and we would rather take the jump voluntarily, to discover other aspects of ourselves, other ways to fill in the hole, to make a little money, maintaining our dignity and pride while surviving off what philosopher-journalist André Gorz called a 'frugal abundance'.[16]

Perhaps it's time for us to get politicised around non-work and subvert the professionalisation of work and life. In opting out, or contesting it from within, perhaps we can create a bit of havoc, refuse to work as we're told, turn demotivation into a positive device – a will to struggle for another kind of work, where use-values outbid exchange values and amateurs trump professionals. If, in times of austerity, capitalists can do without workers, then maybe it's high time workers (and ex-workers) realise that we can do without capitalists, their professional agents and their professional institutions. We can invent work without them, we can perform in other ways for ourselves.

But the problem of *performativity* is stubborn. It eats away inside us, cuts across class and goes up and down the employment ladder, from those performing at the bottom, usually reluctantly and with little motivation, to those at the top who lean in, who imbibe all the business management nonsense and sport tags as 'story strategists', 'futurists' and 'corporate storytellers', proposing 'humanising narratives' for their corporations and organisations.[17] It's a new form of self-presentation, of self-pacification through self-deception, of convincing yourself that what you do is important, like Mae at the Circle.

Performativity encapsulates the rules of the game in the 'reputation economy', an ever-expanding industry of branding and blanding personal identity, an endless anxiety about how you appear to professional audiences, repressing disagreement, falling in with the pleasing conformity of Groupthink and TEDx. As one media entrepreneur put it, 'I change my job title on my LinkedIn every few months and try to see what hits.' It's as if identity is so multiple, so pliable, that it defies any conviction whatsoever. It has absolutely no foundational basis. People's identities have been hollowed out at the core.

What we're seeing all around, enveloping us practically everywhere, is an inauthenticity so widespread that it's now authentically real. Spin is so ubiquitous, so seemingly omnipotent, that most of us are afraid to admit to it. We fear pointing at it and saying, look, there's no substance to our lives anymore, to what we do, to what we read and watch and listen to, even to what we dream.

In the 1940s, Jean-Paul Sartre wondered where negative attitudes about ourselves arose from. It might seem odd today to talk about 'negative' attitudes when so much professional-speak emphasises the positive, the affirmative, thinking big, positive reinforcement, and so on. But could it be that positive posturing is necessary to enable people to live with the awful truth of the lie they're telling themselves, a feature of the self that Sartre calls *bad faith*? 'Bad faith', says Sartre, 'is a lie to oneself, on condition that we distinguish the lie to oneself from lying in general.'[18]

Sartre holds that bad faith can be a normal aspect of life for a great number of people; people can live quite happily in bad faith. Bad faith penetrates so profoundly that it becomes true, like a self-fulfilling prophesy, a prophesy of trying to find self-fulfilment. It's a game one plays with oneself, with one's own self-appearance in society. Take a waiter in a café, says Sartre, in a famous example from *Being and Nothingness*.[19] Today, we're all somehow this waiter, scrambling around for tips, reaping big dividends from 'representing' ourselves to others.

The waiter's movements are quick, precise, Sartre says, a little too precise sometimes, a little too rapid. He bends over a little too eagerly, too solicitously. 'All his behaviour', Sartre reckons, 'seems to us a game.' The waiter applies himself to chaining his movements as if they were mechanisms, one regulating the other; his gestures and even his voice seem to be mechanisms. ... He's playing. But what's he playing? We need not watch long before we can explain it: he is playing at being a waiter in a café. There's nothing there to surprise us ... The waiter in the café plays with his condition in order to realise it.

So, too, do we play with our condition in order to realise it. We model our movements on mechanisms that regulate one another. Our being, Sartre would have said of us, is 'wholly one of ceremony'.

Sartre portrays a bleak social and psychological process: breaking out of bad faith with sincerity, through self-recovery, isn't so simple. When you've succeeded in persuading yourself that bad faith is really good faith, and find that you get rewarded by society's bad faith, you're well on the way to living with yourself, to living with your own inauthentic self. It's the name of the game for professionals, whether they are aware of it or not. Allotted roles have very definite social rules and norms. They determine what waiters should do, how they play, how they act, how we should act.

We have accepted notions of how we all should behave, what we should look like, how we should represent ourselves to the world. These notions get internalised, perpetuated through ritual and routine, through ideology. They 'hail' us into specific categories, interpellate our roles; and usually, willingly or grudgingly, we accept them. We perform as we should. It takes great courage (or folly) to do otherwise, sometimes self-destructive acts of courage, carried out to purge our bad faith, to expel the lie within our own consciousness, to stop performing.

At this point we might return to Alan Harrington and his Crystal Palace. Where Harrington remains correct is in warning us that our dull, deadening routine today is a form of 'method acting', a 'corporate theatre in which all the actors are bit players'.[20] The actor and the professional have much in common, Harrington notes: both live and perform on a stage. But they differ from how the great Russian theatre director Konstantin Stanislavsky might have seen it. For Stanislavsky, the actor's art involves a *projection* of the self into a role; in the Crystal Palace, the self *recedes* into a role. All is performance, and the performance is that of the *team player*.

In the rules of Holacracy, too, the injunction is to perform like a soccer player: you know you must pass to the striker, not because you're friends with them, but because they're in the best position to score. Even if you hate that person, you'll still pass the ball to that *role*. 'This is the grand misconception', Harrington says. 'The "Organisation is all" had led to all the propaganda on the virtues of team play. We must think in teams. But I am always suspicious.' What's needed is the non-team player, someone with an independent inner honesty, someone who affirms the lonely prominence of 'true commitment' – 'otherwise', Harrington says, 'we will have to face up to a bunch of turnips on the payroll.'[21]

Stanislavsky demands inner honesty from his performers; he demands that they become beings 'for-themselves', as the existentialists put it. It's a message we might want to think about. Actors must incarnate their own personalities, build themselves into the character and the role – not simply 'play the part'. As Harrington says, just as a Stanislavskian actor 'pours himself into a role, the Palace executive pours himself *out*'. The easiest way to capitulate to 'playing the part' is to capitulate to routine.

Routine is everything Stanislavsky wants to avoid. 'If we are to embrace life', Harrington says, 'we must ever be on our guard lest routine's deadly roots take hold.' Not to give in to routine means ridding yourself of the other person you're hiding behind, asking those questions Stanislavsky said an actor should constantly ask themselves: Who am I? Why am I here? Where do I come from? And where am I going? But instead of applying them to a role, you apply them to yourself. Harrington says we need some kind of shock of recognition to jolt us out of our routinised professional method acting, to pour ourselves wholeheartedly back into our lives, to no longer be minor characters in the drama, minor team players.

'I think what the Crystal Palace could use right now', he says, 'would be a court jester, a wild card, to upset the order of our days. We could employ a tumbler, a camp joker, even a fool, whose job would be to bring irreverence to our halls.' This court jester

should be permitted to make fun of everybody, great or small, to mock every process (in an irresponsible way), to call a spade a spade, to dramatise errors, to stick his head in conference rooms, interrupt procedures with a wisecrack and vanish again. You would never know when they were coming … The corporation joker would be an irritant to our complacency. Cutting capers across our routine, they wouldn't really disrupt the system. Yet they'd shake it up a bit.

6

Professional Democracy

Participation continues to get touted at work, yet it's been thoroughly purged from political life. Representative democracy has narrowed its circle; fewer and fewer people outside the fold are permitted to enter the spinning doors of parliamentary politics. There's a growing divide between the idea of democracy and its practice. Professionalism has a lot to do with it. Professionalism encircles democracy, draws an enclosure around it, defines what's inside while pushing away what's outside. Within this enclosure, we have a growing distinction between elected politicians and non-accountable technocrats; the latter now overwhelm the former. The trappings of the state are increasingly the domain of a private elite. This is how 'professional' democracy prevails and flourishes; it defines itself through exclusivity, through a *lack* of democracy.

Like a lot of my friends active in politics during the 1980s, I became disillusioned as we passed into the 1990s. This disillusionment really kicked in during the Tony Blair years, even if by then I was living in Bill Clinton's America. Around the millennium, when George W. Bush came to the Oval Office, my disinterest in mainstream politics became total. To this day, I can barely bring myself to listen to any politician, anywhere. I hardly ever read about parliamentary politics in the newspapers, and have no interest in the promises or policies of professional politicians.

It's a terrible thing to admit, especially coming from someone so passionate about politics. I'm still passionate about politics. But nobody in public office speaks the kind of politics that arouses my passions. Most people I know feel the same. Almost everything one hears from those in power sounds feckless or fraudulent. Usually it sounds both feckless *and* fraudulent. It's another act of performance, a political role-playing. And often it's performed very badly, by professionals who seem completely out of touch with the reality of ordinary people. As someone once said of the British Parliament, the only person who ever went there with an honourable intent was Guy Fawkes.

Politicians aren't driven by concerns of morality and equity; their remit is much shallower, more introverted. They respond not to peoples' consciences but to business confidences. They've converted paternalism into directorship, state governance into accountancy dominance. They convene in corporate boardrooms and official chambers far away from any agora, from any openly public forum. Their major motivation seems no more than to reproduce their kind and their privileges. That's why I endorse something Guy Debord said in 1988, in his book *Comments on the Society of the Spectacle*: 'For the first time in contemporary Europe, no party or fraction of a party even tries to pretend that they wish to change anything significant.'[1]

One feature of professionalism is how it has colonised the space between the public and the private, between the state and civil society, between politics and the economy. The state no longer regulates the economy: it has been integrated into the economy. Public well-being is now a pretext for private plunder. The political doors between the public and the private don't just revolve: they spin like washing machines. People charged with protecting public interests are bought and sold without even a pretence of regulation or accountability. Take David Hartnett, head of tax at Britain's HM Revenue & Customs until 2012: his sweetheart deals helped giants like Starbucks and Vodafone avoid paying billions in corporate tax. Now Hartnett works for the accountancy firm Deloitte, whose clients include Vodafone and Starbucks. Meanwhile, the cabinet secretary and head of the civil service, Sir Jeremy Heywood, is the living embodiment of the revolving door, having moved effortlessly from the Treasury to Tony Blair's office then to the investment bank Morgan Stanley and back to work for Tory prime minister David Cameron.

At the same time, public services have been privatised, contracted out in wide-ranging deals brokered by accountancy firms. Not long ago, BBC Radio 4 probed into these murky waters in a documentary called 'The Accountant Kings'. 'The public sector is undergoing a massive transformation', began its reporter Simon Cox. 'Do you know who's running your [Birmingham's] services here? Do you still think it's the council?' Only the clued-up know it's no longer the council but a private company, Capita. 'Capita are doing all the finances, aren't they?' said one of Birmingham's concerned citizens. 'They're controlling all the money.'

Capita, one of a handful of large-scale service providers that now handle many functions of the state, from prisons to the management of benefits, started emptying bins in the 1990s. But today they're a lot more than trash collectors, taking over multiple sectors of local government. Capita is a giant corporation that acts as an Information Technology service provider and call centre operator, as well as a massive refuse collection subcontractor. They dominate municipal public services up and down Britain.

Since 2006, Birmingham has had an outsourcing contract with Capita currently worth £126 million a year. But few councillors have a clue as to how that money is spent. The actual contract document, concocted by accountancy giant Ernst and Young, is crammed with dense price structuring equations, abstruse financial calculations and projections running over 1,000 pages. It's purposefully complex, or so believes Labour councillor John Clancy, designed to be incomprehensible to all but the savviest professional accountant.

Capita's wheelings and dealings are utterly beyond public remit, let alone elected representatives; so, too, are accountancy firms a power unto themselves. 'I've lost control of the future', admits Clancy. It's shocking stuff for a public servant to confess, especially on the record; especially from an official who's since gone on to become leader of Birmingham City Council. 'I can't tell you what Capita told me', adds Clancy,

> because it's the very nature of these contracts that they're bound up in commercial confidentiality. I would love to be able to have a free and open and honest discussion with other councillors and with my electors about this contract. I can't, it's as simple as that. And this is another angle of the nature of these big outsourcing contracts, because they do indeed protect, to a certain extent, trade secrets, pricing structures, which would only work in these contracts, and they are the things that make these contracts make money.[2]

Capita's profit comes at a time when councils are everywhere forced into drastic austerity cuts to save millions of pounds each year. 'I think increasingly I feel that as a citizen', says Trevor Rawles of West Birmingham's East Quinton Citizen Tenant Panel, 'we have no control, and at the moment those elected representatives don't seem to either have the control over the contracts or wish to exert control over the contracts.'

In the 1990s, the French sociologist Pierre Bourdieu called this cleavage within the capitalist state a split between its left and right hands. It's a drama, Bourdieu said, played out between the left hand – a dwindling bunch of frontline elected politicians answerable to their constituents – and the right hand, a 'state nobility' of unelected, unaccountable senior technocrats, financiers and accountants, bankers and lawyers who are not in any way answerable to the needs and desires of ordinary citizens.

Bourdieu says that this left hand and right hand no longer know one another; worse, the right hand no longer wants to know what the left hand does. As budgetary shackles tighten, it no longer gives the left-hand side the chance to do its former job.[3] The rift, Bourdieu says, reflects the 'crisis of politics', a 'civil war' within the state itself, marked by the ever-widening gap between rank-and-file representatives and administrators; between those elected to take public action to improve peoples' lives, and right-leaning, pragmatic senior civil servants who care only about the private, about budgets and bank balances, about cost squeezes.

It's the right hand that leads the professionalisation of politics, the professionalisation of democracy itself, turning it into its own private fiefdom. On this right side, we have a nobility of powerful agents propping up the higher echelons of the ministry of finance and its regime of accountancy governance. This state nobility forms part of a new *rentier* aristocracy, elites who have all the privileges and authority of a nobility, in the medieval sense of the word, and who look upon their authority and privileges as some God-given just reward.

Needless to say, there are plenty of cynical pragmatists on the left hand side of the state, too, just as not everyone on the right side is a heartless civil servant. But what Bourdieu is trying to do here is get a handle on an important struggle that has unfolded at the very core of capitalism. The transformation of the state and the professionalisation of politics reveal the extent of the neoliberal agenda everywhere; what's happened in-house within the capitalist state is thus the basis and the reinforcement of this agenda. It is both its launch pad and its realisation.

Bourdieu was well placed to see this unfold in France during the 1980s and 1990s – throughout the François Mitterrand years, during his reign as a nominally socialist president. Bourdieu wanted to know how come a socialist agenda was so constantly and consistently undermined and betrayed. How come the public interest was systematically thwarted by professional politicians, irrespective of their political persuasion? How come both Right and Left pushed through remarkably similar policies?

Bourdieu taught at Paris's Collège de France, an elite *grande école*. Of peasant stock, hailing from France's south-west, he always had problems with his role as a professional academic, surrounded by the super-privileged. Bourdieu didn't quite have amateurism flowing through his veins; but amateurism at least pricked away at his intellectual conscience later in life.

Many of his ideas on the state were tested out in a public seminar series, open to all comers, conducted over the late 1980s and early 1990s. Bourdieu could have lectured on anything he liked, yet he chose to talk about the state. He thought it politically important. From the piles of notes, annotations, transcripts, photocopies and oral recordings Bourdieu left behind, these lectures have been reconstituted in book form: *Sur l'état*.[4]

In one lecture, Bourdieu suggests that the right hand is a meta-power (*méta-pouvoir*) who has successfully engineered 'a bureaucratic revolution' (*révolution bureaucratique*).[5] In fact, the 'bureaucratic field' now prevails over the 'political field' as such; elite technocrats and bureaucrats dominate the decision-making scene almost everywhere. Representatives in the political field, those who once presided over the 'providential state' – the left-hand side – now cower before their technocratic masters.

The class cleavage is apparent, and in France it runs like a dime crime novel: judges and top civil servants are always posh, conservative, bourgeois and Parisian, whereas police commissioners and cops on the ground, at local stations, like locally elected representatives themselves, come from more lowly stock, from the vicinity, and sound it: they have distinctive regional accents.

Bourdieu never saw himself as a professional *doxo*-intellectual. Thousands of years ago, Plato spoke about *doxosophers* – 'technicians of opinion who think themselves wise'. Bourdieu updates this idea to denote pseudo-intellectual professionals who pontificate eloquently. They're always on TV, produce newspaper columns and TED talks, do anything and everything to promote their works and advance their careers. Their insights are frequently shallow even while they spout highbrow. They know all the soundbites, the media and journalistic clichés, the right words and seductive tropes – the French media is full of *doxo*-intellectuals, and Bourdieu hated them. *Doxo*-intellectuals give ideological and ideational credibility to the right-hand side of the state; they prop it up, give it spin, oil those revolving doors.

Like Edward Said, Bourdieu believed that real scholars should oppose *doxo*-intellectuals because real scholars present themselves critically and questioningly, independently and confrontationally, avoiding mass-media accolades and spotlights. Bourdieu himself was awkward in front of a camera, sometimes deliberately so.[6]

Over the course of the 1990s, as politics drifted towards technocracy, he became increasingly militant. He aligned himself with workers and the *précariat*, with the *sans-papiers*, with the oppressed and dispossessed – with all ordinary amateurs struggling to get by.

In December 1995, during a public-sector walkout, he spoke alongside striking workers outside Paris's Gare de Lyon, condemning the state nobility's slashing of the public budget, its 'destruction of civilisation'.[7] Bourdieu accused the state, under its right-hand auspices, of 'withdrawing from sectors of social life for which it was previously responsible: social housing, public service broadcasting, schools, hospitals, etc. ... What is described as a crisis of politics, of anti-parliamentarianism, is in reality despair at the failure of the state as guardian of the public interest.'

As for the current opposition between the views of an 'enlightened elite' and 'the impulses of the populace', Bourdieu thinks this is typical of reactionary thinking at all times and in all countries. 'But now', he says, 'it takes a new form with the state nobility, which derives the conviction of its legitimacy from academic qualifications and from the authority of science, especially economics.' Not only by divine right, 'but also by reason and modernity does the movement of change lie on the side of these governors – the ministers or "experts"; unreason and archaism, inertia and conservatism are on the side of the people, the trade unions and critical intellectuals.'

Bourdieu insists that democracy must be rescued from technocracy; the latter has kidnapped the state, he says, preached its withering away, made public goods a private fancy, turned passive citizens into active consumers. Ordinary people – ordinary outsiders – must contest the historical inevitability professed by the administrative doyens of neoliberalism, fight them, and, wherever possible, neutralise them.

Bourdieu highlights a distinction lodged at the core of modern representative democracy, a distinction that resides *within* the state, inside its internal chambers and departments. The reality of professional democracy, he's telling us, can frustrate even professional politicians themselves, let alone ordinary people. It's a troubling vision of where our politics is headed, and it reminds me of one of Walter Benjamin's essays on Franz Kafka.

Benjamin wrote this essay in 1934, on the tenth anniversary of Kafka's death.[8] He gets to Kafka by introducing someone called Potemkin, a professional politician, Catherine the Great's chancellor, a drunk and depressive. During one unusually prolonged low, Potemkin retreats to his private chambers. Nobody is allowed in, and nothing can be done without his signature. So official business piles up; policies can't be enacted and grave irregularities result; Russian ministries come to a standstill.

Then, one day, a young minor politician called Shuvalkin struts in. 'What's up?' he wonders. The ministers explain. 'If that's all it is, gentlemen', he replies, 'give me those files, I beg you.' The ministers have nothing to lose. Shuvalkin grabs the bundles of papers and sets off through the galleries, along the corridors, to Potemkin's bedchamber. Without knocking, he marches in, thrusting the documents under the nose of the bedridden chancellor. Dipping his plume in ink, he hands it to Potemkin. Absent-mindedly, sleepily, Potemkin executes the first signature, then a second, then a third, and eventually all of them.

Shuvalkin dashes back to the ministers. They bend over the documents. No one says a word; the group stands frozen. Once again, Shuvalkin approaches; once again he inquires: what is the reason for the gentlemen's consternation? Then his glance falls on the signature. Document after document is signed: 'Shuvalkin, Shuvalkin, Shuvalkin …'

This vignette, says Benjamin, strikes like a messenger, heralding Kafka's work two centuries in advance. Shuvalkin, like Kafka's K., has a brush with authority, is partly assuaged, yet ultimately comes away empty-handed, frustrated by a right-hander. Those right-hand authorities, mysterious and secluded in their bedchambers, in their dark attics within attics, along corridors off corridors, are there, sometimes glimpsed, sometimes even challenged, yet always – or seemingly always – they elude and deflect opposition: their power remains intact come what may.

Ancient paradigms of democracy call for impartial right-hand representation as a ballast to partisan left-hand excess. This is broadly Plato's ideal of democracy. He envisions the rule of smart oligarchs – 'perfect guardians', he calls them in *The Republic* – guided by calm philosophical judgement. They are a sort of moderate right hand of the state who prevent ordinary citizens meddling in the administration of justice, unduly affecting left-handers, stirring up passions and destabilising the strict order of things.

In another of his books, *The Laws*, Plato reaffirms rule coming directly from above, from the top, brooking no dissent. Yet at the same time, he insists on checks and balances, to ensure that the guardians' regime proceeds wisely and fairly. Not a few of these safeguards now seem woefully overlooked, or purposefully forgotten, by those in power. Plato says the guardians have to be elected by the whole citizen body. Citizens must feel they have a stake in the system, that they are not disenfranchised; every official has to be accountable for their conduct, accountable to the people.

Crucial for Plato is a body of 'Scrutineers', overseers of oligarchic power who ensure that this power isn't abused. Imagine, he says, a government scenario, an all-too-familiar government scenario: 'What if one politician proves so inadequate to the dignity and weight of his office that he gets "out of true" and does something crooked?' 'It's desperately difficult', Plato says, 'to find someone of high moral standards to exercise authority over the authorities, so to speak, but try we must.'[9]

Fast-forward several thousand years, when the guardians of our representative democracy assume other controlling roles, less philosophically inspired. The switch from guardianship to directorship, with public servants serving private interests, has been particularly abrupt yet subtle over the past twenty years. In the 1970s, state guardianship was firmly in the hands of elected public representatives. At the municipal level, councillors and administrators undertook guardianship roles; 'urban managers' helped distribute public services to people.

The English sociologist Ray Pahl became fascinated by the functioning of these urban managers, naming a new school of sociological thought after them: *urban managerialism*. By urban managers, Pahl meant planners, councillors, social workers, housing officers and other public sector bureaucrats who affected the whole allocative process around public goods and services. These officials, Pahl said, were 'social gatekeepers' determining people's 'life-chances'.[10]

However flawed this system was, it functioned through a principle of equity, a vague notion of redistributive justice. Urban managers were public servants and should always be kept on their toes. They should always practice fair and just decision-making, which was the political purpose of urban managerialism in the first place: to keep tabs, to scrutinise public servants, to keep them publicly minded, to keep politics public. Communication channels had to stay open. Concerned citizens, Pahl said, 'need to know not only the rates of access to scarce resources and facilities for given populations but also the determinants of the moral and political values of those who control these rates. We need to know how the basic decisions affecting life-chances in urban areas are made.'

But throughout the 1980s and 1990s, the guardians of this urban system began to assume different managerial roles, different controlling duties. They started to recede from public view. They instigated privatisation and the outsourcing of public service delivery. After a while, dabbling with the public budget became babbling: entrepreneurial managers turned into managerial entrepreneurs, and then into middle-management technocrats, each with their own exclusive and private hegemony of meaning. Before long, a new nobility assumed the mantle of political and authoritative power, forming 'a para-state' (as Guy Debord called it); Bourdieu's right-hand side duly emerged, fist clenched.

And nobody bothers keeping tabs anymore. These managers fulfil public duties and undertake public roles, yet do so within a more expansive and invasive private sector. Now, a diverse array of professionals administers the privatisations and sell-offs, calling the economic shots as they draft the private contracts in which the public sector always seems destined to lose out. Now, a hybrid species of public-private sector bureaucrat has evolved, epitomised by the Troika bureaucrats from the European Commission, European Central Bank and International Monetary Fund. These international *fonctionnaires* – for-profit public sector venture capitalists – now determine the life-chances of Europe's crisis zone.

Elsewhere, there are the managers and accountants presiding over Moody's and Standard & Poor's, two private companies that sway the fortunes of cities and regions everywhere, giving 'specialist' financial opinions that define the credit-worthiness of metropolises. One condition for getting the coveted 'AAA' long-term rating (or short-term 'Prime-1' rating) is that the municipality apply the holy writ of accountancy governance, trim its public budget and privatise its infrastructure.

In consequence, city assets have been put on sale and bought up cheaply by another sort of manager, the hedge fund or private equity manager. After preying on wounded corporations over the past decade, this figure now devotes attention to wounded municipalities across America.

Cogsville, a New York-based private equity firm, has been buying up fire-sale and repossessed properties for a while. In 2012, the company bid $11.8 million to win a bulk-buy auction of ninety-four foreclosed homes in Chicago, sold off by the government-controlled mortgage company, Fannie Mae. 'Our belief', said Don Cogsville, CEO of the Cogsville Group, 'is that we acquired these at a decent, sub-market price. I think there's going to be a lot more opportunity there.'[11] In Chicago's Portage Park, Cogsville is the new neighbourhood landlord. Blackstone, another Big Apple firm, owns large swaths of repossessed and knockdown housing stock in Phoenix. Private equity funds such as Cogsville and Blackstone, as well as Oaktree Capital and Colony Capital, have spent around $8 billion to snap up tens of thousands of single-family homes in distressed urban America.

In the 1960s, poor people in America were denied credit. They couldn't get bank loans or financial aid because they earned too little, or lived in the wrong part of town; whole populations and neighbourhoods, invariably minority populations and neighbourhoods, were written off as high-risk or 'redlined', starved of financial support for property ownership and small business development. One of the great popular successes of this era was the implementation of the Community Reinvestment Act of 1977, outlawing redlining practices.

Lately, though, in a cruel twist of fate, in a savage contra-flow, poor people have been showered with loans, frequently at exorbitant rates, with all kinds of hidden fees thrown in. The US's subprime mortgage bubble was hyper-inflated by predatory loans; its bursting entailed foreclosures galore – 3 million, in fact, between January 2007 and August 2010 – and repossessions by lender offenders who eventually got bailed out by the federal government. That's been the cue for hedge funds to step in.

Ordinary citizens would do well to cast a critical eye over the doings of the guardians of our professional democracy. One issue is how the probing amateur today needs to be a sophisticated forensic scientist, a skilled lawyer and an able accountant – if only to keep track of all those professionally negotiated contracts and secret equations, those abstruse tables and reams of legal small print. A major problem, aside from the knowledge base, is the time base. Being a well-intentioned amateur takes up, as Oscar Wilde said, a lot of evenings and weekends, and requires considerable dedication and commitment.

Dedicated amateurs on the *outside* need to get at professionals on the *inside*, force this private inside to be answerable to the public outside. Citizens must access the HQs and centres of technocratic and financial power, lobbying for transparency around what goes on within these citadels of professional democracy. Pressure from the outside, from an amateur undercurrent, might give floating left-handers the courage to step out of the closet, to try to take back democracy from technocracy. This might let reluctant professionals become amateurs again, restore more meaning to what they do, embolden them to become less alienated, less powerless, and, above all, less compliant to their administrative masters.

Resistance from the outside might hook up this inside to the outside. Official representatives in government, in council chambers, in the progressive parties and unions, might be kept on their toes by amateur shouts in the street, by a social movement exerting its pressure from without, in the public square, in alternative media, across clandestine airwaves, forcing the right hand of the state to respond to a reinvigorated left hand.

The emergence of Jeremy Corbyn as Labour Party leader hints at this. People are evidently fed up with post-Blairite spin, with Milibandism, with Tory revanchism. Promising to renationalise public infrastructure, abolish student fees, reverse austerity, curb corporate greed, and reinstate democracy, Corbyn's Old Left line sounds fresh and new to a lot of people, especially the young and hitherto disenfranchised. Many young people love the sixty-something Corbyn, just as they love the seventy-something Bernie Sanders in the US, because both sound like old records; and worn vinyl with the odd scratch is preferable any day to smooth, lifeless, digital autocue.[12]

Since Corbyn became Labour leader in September 2015, hundreds of thousands have signed up to join the Labour Party, mostly younger people and women. On 6 May 2015, the day before Cameron won the General Election, Labour Party membership stood at 201,293; on 10 January 2016, it had risen to 388,407, in what many now call the 'Corbyn effect'.[13] As I write, it has nudged over 500,000. Britain might be witnessing a mini-revival of socialism with a mass base, and with a coherent and convincing set of ideas. But the media is out to get Corbyn. So are right-handers, inside both the Labour and Conservative parties. His most ardent defender is the Momentum group, established in Liverpool by harder-Left supporters. (No surprise there: the city has seen 58 per cent cut from its public budget over the past six years.) Is all this enough to get me re-energised about parliamentary politics? I'm not sure. Perhaps a little.

In the run-up to his leadership battle, Corbyn campaigned for a different paradigm of representative democracy, one pushing for greater participation. On the 'Future of the North', his team emailed every registered Labour supporter in the north of England, inviting ideas for a regional policy. They filtered and compiled the 1,200 replies into a policy document that was then published, inviting further input from supporters and the wider public. This approach is markedly more interesting than recruiting a policy wonk, or McKinsey, or some think tank or panel of 'experts', paying them dearly to formulate barren policy from on high.

Even the way a politician engages with the capitalist media has changed under Corbyn. Professional critics snipe that he comes on like an amateur; it won't last, can't last. Yet somehow it does last, does work, might work better. 'The Labour leader's candid approach', a headline suggested, '... sets fresh challenges for journalists.' (It's always fascinating how honesty can be 'challenging'.) 'He has not been media-trained', they say. A colleague of his retorts: 'The thing about him is he's just authentic ... he knows so much about his subject. It's effective because people can see it's genuine ... he just answers the question. I think the broadcasters have been kind of unhinged by it.'[14]

The Corbyn effect comes hot on the heels of a mini-backlash to the perennial plundering of public services; we've glimpsed this the world over. It's what critics said all along: with outsourcing, service delivery worsens and public costs inflate. And the monies amassed are pocketed as shareholder dividends or executive bonuses, at ordinary taxpayers' expense. In Britain, a few years ago, over half of 140 local councils thought that taking services back from the private sector would be a smart idea. In 2010,

Paris 're-municipalised' its water supply; re-municipalisation isn't the panacea, needless to say, but if nothing else it means greater control by the elected authority, hence greater accountability; citizens can then have some say in running stuff that's crucial for public well-being.

Similar rethinks are happening in Germany with energy distribution networks and waste disposal. Likewise in the Netherlands, Norway, Italy and Belgium. In Britain, Newcastle City Council staved off privatisation of its IT services and refuse collection. The local branch of the public sector workers' union (UNISON) stepped in and helped galvanise a campaign of rank-and-file dissent and outside public pressure on elected insider politicians. The latter eventually relented, passing a resolution for in-house management – 'insourcing' – as proposed by the people. 'The Newcastle experience', says Hilary Wainwright in an aptly titled report called *The Tragedy of the Private, The Potential of the Public*, 'takes our thinking about democratisation further, opening up and democratising the normally hidden, taken-for-granted internal process of managing public resources.'[15]

'Public-public partnerships' offer another democratic paradigm of collective consumption provision, a new moment of opportunity. Public-public partnerships underwrite an inspiring initiative in Norway, spearheaded by the Norwegian municipal public workers' union, Fagforbundet. The enemy has been the familiar privatisation of public services; yet the union has been unusually visionary and ambitious in mobilising its amateur base, transforming the internal organisation of public administration through a 'Model Municipality Experiment'. Public sector workers have developed enough collective muscle that they've been able to participate alongside official representatives in service delivery decision-making. Well-organised amateur outsiders can participate as insiders, and creative ways can be engineered to balance urban budgets and equitably redistribute services – rather than hand them over to capital for private exploitation.

There's a sense that the philosophy might be changing; changing because of public outcry, because amateurs want more engaged participation in public decision-making, because the deeper question of 'public values' is now getting debated. At the same time, many have started to look askance at remote right-handers in our midst, at non-accountable technocrats, the European Commission, experts and policy wonks, at an entrenched political 'establishment'. Fingers have been pointed from across the entire political spectrum, from the far Left to the far Right. And much finger-wagging has gone on in between.

Now, the common thread throughout is people's recognition of their own disenfranchisement. It's reached desperate depths. But frustration compounded by vulnerability has enabled assorted demagogues to step in. Some have voiced populist raging against the machine, created scapegoats galore, any old or new straw target, anything to further their vested interests and ambitions. They've had it in for both right and left hands of the state. And a lot of listeners, for want of an alternative, have believed them.

And yet, even with so much bad faith poisoning political culture, sometimes you need to emphasise the good faith. The doubling of Labour Party membership under Corbyn, the rallying support of millions of Americans for Bernie Sanders, the anti-establishment mood across Europe and the US, suggest that cracks are appearing in the thin veneer of professional democracy; that the right hand is now on the back foot. This anti-establishment mood has unleashed a renewed spirit of confrontation. If nothing else, the message is that enough is enough, that a different sort of politics, with different values, is not only warranted but entirely justified. Here we even have a vision of a politics that is *political* again: conflictual, heated, angry. It's a piercing call to straddle the representative–participatory divide, to leap across what has for so long been a deep and dark abyss.

Such a vision of politics is encouraging, too, because it suggests that the state isn't an impenetrable bloc. Rather, it's riven with cracks and contradictions. These cracks and contradictions are moments of opportunity and possibility. The issue isn't to have a professional bourgeois state on the one side, and its democratic nemesis, the people, rank amateurs, on the other – the 'dual power' thesis, which Lenin advocated before the Bolshevik Revolution. Democracy is a more fluid reality, fluid between the state's right and left hands, fluid between its professional and amateur protagonists.

Democracy, in other words, is a double action, not a dual power. It's about sufficient outsiders and comradely insiders getting together to overwhelm the inside. Inner struggle within the state has to express itself alongside popular pressure outside the state; it's never a simple opposition between 'internal' and 'external' struggle. In any progressive, participatory future, these two forms must be combined. Out of the mix there might arise a democratic state responsive to the needs of people. Maybe even responsive to the needs of people's amateurism.

A few years ago the Norwegian city of Bergen set up an 'Amateur Culture Council', 'an umbrella organisation for everyone who does cultural activities in their spare time'. It's there, official, to help strengthen amateur culture and integrate it into the city's social infrastructure. The Amateur Culture Council is present at municipal meetings, and provides guidance for groups and individuals who try to start up new cultural and arts endeavours. 'We help our organisations find suitable premises and give orientation with regard to grant schemes ... We facilitate meetings between different cultural expressions, the mutual exchange of experiences and ideas, and the establishment of new contacts.' Who can join? 'All cultural organisations active in amateur culture and/or conducting their main activities in volunteer cultural fields may become members.' At last, something worth voting for ...

7

The Genius of Curiosity

The greatest put-down of the expert comes from an unlikely source: 'The Painter of Modern Life', an essay by Charles Baudelaire, published in 1863. This set piece on art and modernity has been celebrated for many things, but it's rarely acknowledged for what I think it is: a supreme evocation of intellectual amateurism and critique of professional expertise.

The amateurism in question is that of a 'singular man', Baudelaire says, who seeks no approval from anybody. He's the nemesis of what constitutes 'success' today. He never puts himself or his work up for tender. His art is truly independent; he signs his pictures only with his soul. In fact, this person wishes to remain incognito, and doesn't want Baudelaire to use his name. 'When he heard that I was proposing to make an assessment of his mind and talent, he begged me, in a most peremptory manner, to suppress his name, and to discuss his works only as though they were the works of some anonymous person.'[1] So Baudelaire calls him simply M. G. – for Monsieur Guys, Constantin Guys, the painter of modern life, the shadowy Other of the expert of modern life.[2]

But Guys wasn't just a painter, nor even an artist. He wasn't a professional specialist whose 'conversations are limited to the narrowest of circles'. Guys was something more: 'a man of the world', Baudelaire says, a 'world-minded' person, of the 'whole world'. Guys can't stand being called a 'specialist', even hates the label of 'artist'. He hates to be tied down to an expertise like a serf to the soil, or an accountant to their accounts. Guys wants to know everything, understand everything, appreciate all that happens on planet Earth, its mysteries and miseries, its delights and disruptions. He wants to embroil himself in everything, to depict in paint on canvas, in pencil and charcoal on paper, in watercolours. How can somebody so open be an expert, a hired hand?

Guys is passionate about passion. Baudelaire searches for appropriate words and finds just the right title for Guys: 'a spiritual citizen of the universe'.[3] This means to celebrate oneself as part of a much bigger reality, with a vaster horizon, to affirm this horizon and not be afraid of its immensity as one's home address. It's the same spirit that lets Joyce's young Stephen Dedalus locate himself in a larger-than-life world: 'Clongowes Wood College, Sallins, County Kildare, Ireland, Europe, the World, the Universe'.

All of this is far removed from today's reality, our cult of expertism, which is more akin to the blasé attitude that Guys detests: the self-righteous certainty of knowing it all, of keeping your horizons wilfully narrow because inside resides your intellectual expertise. Guys scorns the posture of knowing everything, of having seen and done everything, and would be just as damning of those who are content to be consulted and paid because they know everything. So much of what goes on in public life nowadays is blasé, the unimpressionable domain of think-tank wonks and business graduates, of professional know-all experts. This would be anathema to Guys, and to Baudelaire. Both try to keep intact a vision of romantic openness, a fugitive wisdom that seems more vitally needed now than ever before.

Baudelaire's masterwork is *Les Fleurs du mal* – *Flowers of Evil* – a hundred-odd bittersweet poems, first appearing in 1857. Baudelaire kept adding new verse, and a definitive edition of *Les Fleurs du mal* appeared in 1868, a year after the poet's death. A recurring theme of *Les Fleurs du mal* is the psychological and physical loneliness of Baudelaire's great muse – Paris – with its voluptuous atmosphere, a dreamscape in which monsters lurk around every corner. The themes of 'Spleen' and 'Ideal' perpetually oscillate; Baudelaire tries to conquer spleen, reaches out to art, to love, searches for his ideal. Yet spleen continually torments. (Victor Hugo said that *Les Fleurs du mal* 'gives us a new kind of shudder'.)

Walter Benjamin was as fascinated by Baudelaire as I am, perhaps even more so. He suggested that Baudelaire wasn't just an alienated late-Romantic dreamer, but a social poet. Baudelaire understood the forces creating a modern urban capitalism, Benjamin said. He understood how the personal had inevitably become political, and how individuality is willy-nilly caught up in the maelstrom of modern life. It was a new, thoroughly modern paradox: immense freedom, on the one hand, and mass enslavement to commodity culture, on the other. Not for nothing did Benjamin label Baudelaire 'a lyric poet in the era of high capitalism'.[4]

Baudelaire didn't consider poetry a job, nor his *métier*, even if he sometimes got paid to do it. He'd gladly have done it for nothing, and frequently did do it for nothing. He knew that under high capitalism there weren't too many job openings for humanist poets. There are probably less now than there were then. For the artist it's always a relentless struggle to earn a living. Estimates reckon that during twenty years of literary labour, Baudelaire received 10,000 francs, about £1,300. One of his first published pieces set the tone of this struggle, a satirical essay, salted by prose poems: 'How You Pay Your Debts when You've Got Genius'.[5]

Baudelaire never regarded himself as a *professional* poet or critic. This wasn't so much self-deprecation as self-affirmation, a neat sidestep to unaccommodated and unco-opted amateurism, a free-floating outsiderhood. To survive, Baudelaire ducked and dived inside modernity, constructed assorted postures, from provocateur to dandy, seducer to moralist. And although he wrote in what seems like unbearable solitary confinement, his work was always destined for a wider, popular public. Many poems weren't written for learned literary reviews but featured as Op-Eds in *Le Figaro*. They were the *feuilletons* of a roving reporter, episodes of modern vagabondage seen through the eyes of a modern vagabond poet. Nothing could compare today. They were provocations rather than pacifications, partisan and political rather than paltry and platitudinous.

'The Painter of Modern Life' was written as a three-part *feuilleton* for *Le Figaro*. Its most suggestive section is called 'The Artist, Man of the World, Man of Crowds, and Child'. The rubric's ordering marks a subtle shift in logic, a shift of amateur logic – though no less rigorous for it. The shift from the artist as a specialist to man of the world, and thence to man of the crowd and to child, loosens the grip any expert could ever hope to secure on reality and truth.

It took one amateur, Baudelaire, to recognise another, his *semblable*, in Guys. Baudelaire is the painter of the painter of modern life. He's an artist who wrote art criticism for pleasure, about artists like Guys who often painted and drew for pleasure. But Guys, like Baudelaire, burned with serious intensity. They had a whole secret society inside their heads. Baudelaire recounts late one evening when he calls on Guys in his workshop. 'Whilst others are sleeping', Baudelaire writes, this man is leaning over his table, his steady gaze on a sheet of paper, exactly the same gaze as he directed just now at the things about him, brandishing his pencil, his pen, his brush, splashing water from the glass up to the ceiling, wiping his pen on his shirt, hurried, vigorous, active, as though he was afraid the images might escape him, quarrelsome though alone, and driving himself relentlessly on.[6]

It's a lovely evocation of the artist at work, the man of the world in his world. The next day, Baudelaire continues,

when, as he wakes up, M. G. opens his eyes and sees the sun beating vibrantly at his window-panes, he says to himself with remorse and regret: 'What an imperative command! What a fanfare of light! Light everywhere for several hours past! Light I have lost in sleep! And the endless number of things bathed in light that I could have seen and have failed to!' And off he goes! And he watches the flow of life move by, majestic and dazzling.

Guys' point of departure, Baudelaire tells us, is something extremely important for the man of the world, just as it is for the amateurs of our world today. The starting point of his genius is *curiosity*.

Guys, like Baudelaire, had a lust for life that was always curious, forever on the look-out for the new. They didn't seek to affirm themselves through what they already knew; their quest was the *unknown*, 'the inestimable value of novelty'. For Guys, 'curiosity had become a compelling, irresistible passion'. Baudelaire could have easily said this about himself. Curiosity isn't about offering answers, or preaching sure truths, so much as asking questions, wondering why and how come. Curiosity has a double meaning: to treat diligently and with care, and to scrutinise things that are hidden and in some sense don't matter. But it's the things that are supposedly insignificant that often pique one's curiosity. To be curious is to endlessly explore, and to not always find. It might even be as Samuel Beckett says in *Worstward Ho*: 'Try again. Fail again. Fail better.'

Guys may have painted dandies and *flâneurs*, but as Baudelaire makes clear, Guys wasn't either character himself. The dandy and *flâneur* aspire to cold detachment, to indifferent restraint, rather like today's experts, who are consulted for their passionless pragmatism. The expert's nonchalance is one of numbers and metrics, hiding behind PowerPoint, coolly voicing 'facts' not opinions. Experts are only demonstrative with data and deliverables; they are, like Baudelaire's dandy, blasé 'as a matter of policy'. It isn't that amateurs would necessarily do a better job than experts; it's more that what makes experts dangerous is their blasé attitude, their *lack of curiosity*.

Spiritual citizens of the universe are hot rather than cold. They are 'perpetually in the condition of the convalescent'. *Convalescence* is a strange term that Baudelaire borrows from Edgar Allan Poe. Baudelaire had written appreciatively about the Baltimorean poet and critic in 1852, in the *Revue de Paris*. In the mid-1850s, he'd translated Poe's 'Raven', as well as *Tales of Mystery and Imagination*, finding a striking fraternity, a shared temperament, similar ideas about life and art. Convalescence means taking stock after an illness that has shaken you to your existential core, a near-death experience. It's the shock of recognition, a born-again realisation of who you really are. 'Merely to breathe was enjoyment', says Poe's convalescent in 'The Man of the Crowd'. 'I felt a calm but inquisitive interest in everything.' But Baudelaire pushes Poe's convalescence further. He says it's like 'a return to childhood', a progression through regression, seeing everything once more as an infant sees, as we all once saw: with freshness, and a perception that is 'acute and magical'.

The child, Baudelaire says, is always 'drunk'. Children drink in all colours and shapes. One of the first words a child utters, and continues to utter until they learn otherwise, is *why*. Why this, why that? The world is mysterious and they want to comprehend it, to gulp it down. Baudelaire urged adults 'to get drunk', to recapture that childlike wonderment, or else never lose it. 'One should always be drunk. That's all that matters', he said. 'That's our one imperative need ... But with what? With wine, with poetry, or with virtue, as you choose. But get drunk.'[7] Find your passion, intoxicate yourself with it, keep exploring it, wondering, being curious. That's what Baudelaire seems to be telling us, 'so as not to feel the horrible burden of Time that breaks your shoulders and pulls you down'.

Genius, says Baudelaire, is 'no more than childhood recaptured at will, childhood equipped with an adult's physical means to express itself, and with the analytical mind that enables it to bring order into the sum of experience, involuntarily amassed'. What else is this but the restlessness of the amateur? 'To this deep and joyful curiosity must be attributed that stare', Baudelaire says, 'animal-like in its ecstasy, which all children have when confronted with something new, whatever it may be: faces or landscape, light, gilding, colours, watered silk, enchantment of beauty.'[8]

Baudelaire urges us to think of Guys as a 'man-child', as a 'man possessing at every moment the genius of childhood'. Guys is an 'eternal convalescent'. His edge on life will never get blunted. His passion for seeing and feeling everything diverges from dandyism. His most passionate passion – Guys' 'profession', Baudelaire calls it – is 'to merge with the crowd' (*épouser la foule*), to see and feel the elemental passions of ordinary modern life as it is actually lived – for better or for worse. The crowd is Guys' domain. He wants to set up his dwelling in the throng, in the ebb and flow, in the bustle of urbanity, in what is both 'fleeting and infinite'. Guys wants to be away from home yet feel at home everywhere. Guys moves into the crowd as though into 'an immense reservoir of electricity'. He's an 'amateur of life', Baudelaire says, in a memorable phrase, and 'amateurs of life make the whole world their family'.[9]

The amateur of life embraces the whole world, engages in what Baudelaire calls 'universal communion', human empathy and community of an earthly, secular kind. It is down below, in the crowd, that 'an ego athirst' can have its fill, sating itself with 'the non-ego'.[10] Baudelaire quotes M. G. as saying, 'in one of those talks he rendered memorable by the intensity of his gaze, and by the eloquence of his gesture, "Any man … who is bored in the midst of the crowd, is a fool! A fool! And I despise him!"'

We can perhaps grasp here why neither Baudelaire nor Guys would think too highly of the expert, of anybody who tries to stand aloof from the crowd or sees themselves as intellectually superior to the masses. Such people have to get out of their conference rooms and see beyond the flip charts and spreadsheets. Their gaze is remote and looks down upon; it's not an immersion *in*. It's there to tell, not to find out. Experts parachute into distant lands for just a few days. World Bankers 'advise' about infrastructure or governance; callow consultants at McKinsey, with its 'global research and information professionals', collect and collate data online, from afar, wading into projects they have little experience of or *feel* for, notwithstanding their degrees and doctorates.

These experts need to give up their 'halos', Baudelaire would have said, see ordinary life, and learn. 'Scenes of high life and of the thousands of uprooted lives that haunt the underworld of a great city', Baudelaire wrote, 'are there to show us that we have only to open our eyes to see and know the heroism of our day.'[11] Paris is rich in poetic and wonderful subjects, and the marvellous envelops and saturates us everywhere – 'But we fail to see it'. Our idea of the epic is usually more epic. Our idea of history is an 'official' history, embodied in facts and figures. Part of the problem of seeing contemporary heroism is getting out there to see it, having the curiosity to want to see it, and the imagination to make something of it. Baudelaire places imagination on much the same plane as curiosity. The two sensibilities go hand in hand, inspire and feed off each other. He calls imagination 'the queen of the faculties'.

Baudelaire devotes considerable attention to the theme of the imagination in his account of the 'Salon of 1859'. With typical irony, Baudelaire takes to task those professional artists who pander to the industry and merely want to 'copy nature'. 'These doctrinaires', he says, 'are completely satisfied by Nature'. But someone with imagination might instead declare: 'I consider it useless and tedious to represent what exists, because nothing that exists satisfies me.'[12] Somebody with imagination might ask something more philosophical, something more probing: whether the doctrinaires in question 'are quite certain of the existence of *external* nature, or (if this question might seem too well calculated to pander to sarcasm) whether they are quite certain of knowing *all nature*?' A 'yes', Baudelaire says, 'would be the most boastful and extravagant of answers'. Indeed, he adds, we must believe that such pedants 'simply meant to say, "We have no imagination, and we decree that no one else is to have any either."'

How mysterious imagination is, Baudelaire exclaims, how it arouses and provokes, how it has created the world. Isn't it proper, then, that it should govern the world, too? 'Imagination first taught us the moral meaning of colour, of contour, of sound and scent. In the beginning of the world it created analogy and metaphor. ... It creates a new world, it produces the sensation of newness'.[13] There is nothing more formidable than a fine imagination for 'disposing of an immense armoury of observed facts'. Baudelaire reckons that imagination 'supplements' nature and 'embraces also the critical spirit'. To give up on your imagination is to become 'timid and servile', he proclaims, 'to conform to a purely conventional set of rules – rules entirely arbitrary, not derived from the human soul, but simply imposed by routine'.[14]

One of Baudelaire's central insights about imagination is that it gives you the power to imagine *yourself*. Imagination can help us grow up by keeping us young. It can help us evolve, go forth into maturity. We can use imagination to work on ourselves, make an imaginative leap into the world, imagine ourselves in an expansive reality full of wonderment. Baudelaire says that 'imagination has a positive relationship with the infinite'. So imagine how great it could be if we used this queen of faculties to push beyond the prison-house of facts.

With imagination, we could be faithful to ourselves rather than to routine, break out of convention, uphold a vision of poetic excitement about ourselves and our world. The visible universe is but a storehouse of images and signs, Baudelaire says, that 'imagination must digest and transform'. With imagination, we can invent our own heroism of modern life. The Baudelairean hero always tries to jerk themselves out of the apathy of routine, for the will to 'escape' lies deep at the core of the human heart. To be free, Baudelaire says, is to live with intensity. Intensity contests the actuality of existing reality. But the actuality of existing reality also works against intensity of experience, tries to stifle it, to tame it. This is why Baudelaire indicted his age, and why he would indict ours.[15]

There have been moments in my life when I have needed Baudelaire badly. When I have felt isolated and marginalised, reading him I felt less isolated and marginalised. Soon I even began to enjoy and affirm my isolation and marginalisation. When things get dramatic, Baudelaire helps you self-dramatise and feel better. I have dreamily followed Baudelaire often, dressed in black like him, gloomily wandering about some city or another, mingling with its phantom underworld.

> I go out alone to practice my fantastical fencing,
> Scenting chances for rhyme on every street corner,
> Stumbling over words as though they were cobblestones,
> Sometimes knocking up against verses dreamed long ago.
>
> And who knows whether my dreams' new flowers
> Will find within this soil, washed like a shore,
> The mystic nourishment that would make them strong.[16]

Baudelaire's gloominess is something to rejoice in. Somebody once asked him why he always dressed in black, why so mournful? His black frock-coat, he said, was 'the expression of the public soul'. And besides, 'all of us are attending some funeral or another'.

Such a spirit fits awkwardly into a professional environment. Baudelaire is playful with ambiguity. His amateurism is comic and ironic. His ambiguities don't imply uncertainty, they convey honesty; they don't lack clarity, but express tension. He is the peripatetic antidote to the established occupational role, to the conventional box or mould. Once you are in a mould, it is hard to break out. It is much harder to become an amateur of life than an expert of life. On the other hand, it's perhaps hardest of all for experts to break out of their moulds. They've constructed an iron cage around themselves in which they're at once the warders and the inmates. A lot has to do with the 'Reputation Economy', the marketing and industrialising of your identity, the branding of your specialist skills, exploiting the cult of likability to win clients. But could we ever envisage Baudelaire or Guys caring about their public reputation?

University academics are pressed by their administrative masters to produce their own repertoire of unambiguous soundbites. They appear on their institution's 'Directory of Experts', a searchable database of the 'Research Expertise' of every faculty member. We find a scholar's intellectual profile whittled down to a half-dozen expertise keywords, a peculiar branding peddled by all universities and 'Centres of Excellence'. How to judge the most excellent amidst all this excellence? Which expert out of an endless roster of experts? Who is the most expert expert?

If you want to search a little deeper – or maybe more shallowly – into the brave new world of experts, you can consult 'The Academy of Experts', a 'professional body for experts to establish and promote high objective standards'. (Though we might enquire what 'objective' means.) Here you can leverage your expertise, get hired, or hire an expert yourself. The London-based academy, founded in 1987, 'is both a professional society and a qualifying body which provides, for the first time, a single source of qualified, independent experts experienced in a wide range of professional, commercial and industrial disciplines from around the world'. There are comprehensive training courses to develop expertise as 'Mediators', 'Conciliators' and 'Expert Determiners'.

Once you're on the expert listing, though, you're usually stuck with it. Once an expert always an expert. You are typecast. Moving in and out of categories, if ever the desire should strike you, is a tricky affair. Disciplinary border controls and intellectual gatekeepers won't grant security clearance, won't let you into unknown intellectual territories, other thought-spaces where you have no reputation, no qualifications. Expertise frustrates genuine interdisciplinarity and inquisitive learning, muffles curiosity. It crushes imaginative flair, ignores the pure joy of not knowing what you're doing, of zigzagging and fumbling around a subject until you master it. That's the real route to expertise: it's a process that lasts a lifetime, not a product you buy from a training course.

Still, confronted with this hegemony of the expert, the amateur will always have their work cut out. To embrace amateurism, says Baudelaire, is a '*damnation* already done'. Amateurism will be your joy, for sure, but also your eternal curse, your perpetual challenge. It will be both diabolical and divine. It'll be your mutiny in search of personal authenticity, your quest to tell the truth about yourself in a society that rewards you for telling lies, for playing its game. Baudelaire is inviting us to join him on a voyage, condemning us forever to be accomplices in his haunting ideal.

8

Hobby-Horse

One of my favourite pieces on identity politics is a children's story: *Rumpelstiltskin*, a Brothers Grimm adaptation of a tale that goes back 4,000 years. I have read it many times with my young daughter. We love best Tony Ross's illustrated take on a goblin who gets a bad rap.[1] The goblin is seen as the villain, while the real perpetrators – the miller, his daughter, and the king – are presented as good and upright; it's they who live happily ever after. But Rumpelstiltskin, the goblin, is the only honest soul amongst them, the only character true to his word. The older I get, the more I've come to identify with Rumpelstiltskin, and connected him to where I've come from. Perhaps hailing from Liverpool helps you sympathise with outsiders, with peripheral people, with goblins? Perhaps it helps you recognise how ideological this story actually is? The goblin isn't interested in money or status. So why is it that society has our kids identify with the king, the father and the daughter, who are?

The miller is a liar who gives away his daughter to the king. The miller says she can spin straw into gold, which of course she can't. The king, who's nasty and greedy, is impressed. He carts her off and locks her up in a dungeon with a spinning wheel. If she can turn the piles of straw into gold then he'll marry her; if not, it's off with her head. The king is excited at the prospect of so much wealth and will stop at nothing to get it. 'I'll be back in the morning for the gold', he says. As night falls, the girl is at a loss living up to her father's conceited promise. She starts to cry.

Suddenly, a funny little goblin appears, asking the reason for her tears. He listens with a sympathetic ear. After she explains, he laughs. 'Is that all? Why, I can do that in a twinkle', he says nonchalantly. For him, you don't have to be very clever to spin lots of gold (they do it all the time on the stock market, spinning yarns all the way to the bank); nor do you have to work particularly hard. Rumpelstiltskin knows that making lots of money is no big deal, that there are other paradigms to life, other less venal and more magical ways to find fulfilment. He spins the gold in return for the girl's pretty necklace. Next morning, the king is delighted. That evening, Rumpelstiltskin returns and spins more gold, this time in exchange for the girl's ring. The king, again, is thrilled. On the third evening, the miller's daughter has nothing more to give the goblin, so she promises him her first-born child. This time, he fills the whole room with gold, and the king goes wild with excitement and marries the girl that very same day.

The kingdom rejoices at the marriage and later at the birth of the queen's beautiful daughter. When the goblin hears the news, he comes back for the baby. 'Remember', he says, 'there was an agreement, and you're bound by that.' The queen weeps, goes down on her knees, begs him not to take her baby away. Again, the goblin sympathises, and says, 'All right, my name is unusual, if you can guess it you're released from the promise.' He'll be back tomorrow, he says.

But the queen plays crooked and sends a servant to snoop and find out his name. A while later, the servant returns, grinning all over. 'I followed him to a little shack, deep in the forest, and there I heard him singing his song, and he bawled out his name.' Next morning, the goblin reappears before the queen. She utters his name and, 'spitting and squealing, he vanished out of the window like a balloon when you take your fingers off the nozzle.' Nothing is ever heard of him again; the king, the queen, and the young princess live happily ... blah, blah, blah.

This warped and shallow value system is inculcated in us early. If you follow its rules, you get rewarded accordingly; you'll live happily ever after. But the reality of the tale is that its winners do everything we know a ruling class does: they lie and cheat, boast and break deals; they even spy on you if need be, and send others to do their dirty work. They don't keep their word. The queen breaks her compact. The king has no other interest than accumulating wealth; he doesn't even love the woman he married. Everybody is duplicitous and conniving. They're all phoney schemers, out to extract something from somebody else – all except the ugly goblin Rumpelstiltskin.

But their devious ways are seen as the straight, respectable way that leads to success, unlike the honest, if harsh, goblin's way. They are society's role models. Theirs is the normal life journey, the expected, anticipated road, the reality that professionals endorse and underwrite.

The rites of passage of 'professional' life start early and are implanted in your brain even when you're being read to at night. It takes enormous strength to beg to differ, to try to expose what's implicit in the message, enormous strength from parents who deviate from the straight and narrow themselves. The straight and narrow path starts early, in childhood, and continues beyond, never stops continuing. At every step, you're forced to choose what appears to be the 'good' and to comply with the 'success-ful'; it's the only guarantee of living happily ever after. Goblins are losers.

I never bought into the straight and narrow way. I was a loser. I screwed up at school, was hopeless, failed everything – well, almost: I got a couple of CSEs, as I remember – and quit Quarry Bank school, John Lennon's alma mater, at sixteen, with no idea what I wanted to do with my life, unenthused by the prospect of work. I didn't want to be a rock star or a comedian or a footballer as you're supposed to be, coming from Liverpool. It was partly the school's fault, because later on, after I got out, I discovered a talent that had never been encouraged there; no career service ever spotted it, no teacher paid attention to my lateral-thinking mind. I loved to write, loved to read, loved to write about things I'd read, about things I'd done and people I'd met. But I loved to write about things in a weird way; nothing of the sort ever appeared on any curriculum I was taught. None of this was encouraged at home, either, because while my parents were both loving, there were never any books around the house. My father never read; my mother, rarely. They mostly worked, doing factory shifts between them (one at an engineering works, the other at a pharmaceuticals company, both in Speke). They left school at twelve because of the war.

That passion might've always been there, I don't know. But maybe nobody bothered with me at school because it seemed I wasn't bothered at school. It was 1976: I entered the adult world to seek my misfortune, like the lonely Rumpelstiltskin, just as the Sex Pistols' debut hit, 'Anarchy in the UK', was released, just as economic crises hit hard. This was an era of growing up absurd, of psychological alienation and industrial annihilation; and the Sex Pistols' mantra of NO FUTURE seemed bang on for my own personal manifesto. 'What's the point?' Johnny Rotten asked. I didn't see the point. I followed the goblin way.

The decade was dramatised by a sense of lost innocence; my adolescence dissipated into the damp Liverpool air, into a monotone grey upon grey. I was damned, but also it might've been a lucky escape. How could anyone plan this? How could I plot in advance such a crooked course of self-discovery and self-torment? How could I have known what lay in store? It took me a while to find myself. It took a lot of fumbling around, a lot of anguish and pain; and it is always negotiable, always somehow unfinished, always getting worked through.

In a way, I'm still trying to find myself, and that's one of the reasons for writing this book. Life's elemental movement is the zigzag, meandering about to find your passion, discovering what the eighteenth-century English author Laurence Sterne called your 'Hobby-Horse', something that turns your interest on, that fills your sky, that lights your fire. A 'Hobby-Horsical matter' follows a curious course, Sterne says, an amateur's path of discovery, of perpetual learning, never reaching completion. Sterne was another writer of fairy tales, decades before the Brothers Grimm, a writer of grown-up fairy tales.

In *The Life and Opinions of Tristram Shandy*, published in nine volumes between 1759 and 1767, Sterne declares that the wisest adults have their Hobby-Horse, 'their coins and cockle-shells, their drums and trumpets, their fiddles, their pallets, their maggots and butterflies'.[2] A Hobby-Horse is something we ride passionately, something that gives us the greatest delight imaginable. Sterne isn't thinking about material riches, valuable treasure like gold we can spin from straw. The Hobby-Horse cherished by Uncle Toby, one of his main characters, is reconstructing the 1692 Siege of Namur on the Shandy estate's bowling green. Gentle and fanciful,

Uncle Toby is more interested in miniature war games than in real-life – and real-death – games of war.[3] A Hobby-Horse isn't so much a professional vocation as an amateur avocation, 'an any thing', Sterne says, 'which a man makes a shift to get a-stride on'. With a Hobby-Horse, we meander life's course. We don't tread the straight and narrow.

The straight line is a simple succession of notes, the same notes. It's unmusical. But Sterne sketches the wavering human line: coiled and curvaceous, whimsical and musical, arabesque and affecting, just like life itself. The rhythm of life and of consciousness is digressive and discontinuous, looping and lolloping, reflecting life's mishaps and jolts, its bumps and fidgets. In one vignette from *Tristram Shandy*, Corporal Trim, praising the trail of the free person, flourishes his walking stick, whirling it haphazardly through the air, around and around. Sterne even draws this squiggly line for us all to see vividly, just in case we can't imagine it in our heads, or follow it in our lives. It's a dancing trajectory that defies the spirit of calculation, denies life as logical induction, refuses to go straight for the goal, without detours or delays – the professional Ivy League way, the successful way.

Tristram Shandy is full of diagrams of windy lines mapping the twisted and tormented narrative of Tristram's life story, much of which is recounted before he is born! Such are the digressive paths that a donkey might take, that low-tech, thoroughly amateur beast who stubbornly bears his load through life and who has so often fascinated me.[4] We might recall how the messy dissidence of the donkey disrupts the ordered linearity of such a consummate professional as Le Corbusier, the famous architect and planner: 'Man walks in a straight line', wrote Le Corbusier in the 1920s in *The City of Tomorrow*, 'because he has a goal and knows where he's going.' But 'the pack-donkey meanders along, meditates a little in his scatter-brained and distracted fashion, zigzagging in order to avoid large stones, or to ease his climb, or to gain a little shade.' Ruling classes hate the zigzag.

The zigzag implies uncertainty, that you don't know things in advance, that you can't see exactly where you're headed or where you want to head. You certainly can't see it at sixteen or seventeen, when you're forced to choose your GCSEs and A-Levels; when you're forced to specialise, forced to anticipate what you'll do at university, what you're going to do for your career, for the rest of your life. It's a terrifying prospect. Already, society's trench has been dug out for you. Inevitably, you're compelled to go along with it, to follow its straight course; and it's hard to clamber out, to wander off track, if only to see what somewhere else is like, to experience how it feels. Instead, we do as we ought, like we're expected to. As we grow up, we're already programmed to perform, at school, on the job, in life. We've rehearsed our allotted lines, memorised and normalised them.

Some people find their Hobby-Horse. They tinker away as proud and impassioned amateurs, devoting their spare time at weekends, in the evenings, to messing about in the garage with their tools, digging and planting on the allotment, tending their cherished garden, preparing lavish meals in the kitchen, playing or singing in a band, at a social club, in the pub. Their Hobby-Horse is a private affair, sometimes a secret passion, even if occasionally it's ridden in public. It frequently has nothing to do with their job, and that's why they love doing it, doing it well – or badly. There are many who have found their Hobby-Horse in spite of their jobs, sometimes in spite of their high-powered and highly-paid professional jobs.

How many lawyers in Britain have found their true calling as bakers, competing in the popular TV series *The Great British Bake Off*? The programme has been cathartic for aspiring home cooks, who have discovered their vocation through dedicated amateurism. This is how these people express themselves, test themselves, become technically proficient, even achieve quiet greatness. Yet they do so as amateurs. It seems that professions like law leave a lot of qualified professionals cold. They pay well and bestow high status, but are great dullers of the senses. The activities involved seem to preclude real meaning and intimacy, real creative expression.

Many people might actually love laying bricks, installing plumbing or electrical systems, teaching and designing, lecturing and researching, fiddling around with car engines, driving a truck. But the problem here is that this love isn't a Hobby-Horse: it's a *job*. And it's this that spoils everything. It isn't the content of what they do that's the problem so much as the *form* of how they do it, the context of their work: the organisation, the company, the boss, the demands placed upon employees, the speeds they have to beat, the tasks they have to achieve, the rapidity and intensity of work, its duration and duress.

That's what weighs down on people. That's what evacuates any affection you might have for the activity itself. The job, in simple terms, transforms a labour of love into a loathing of labour. The job introduces a compulsion; you can lay bricks so long as you lay so many per hour; you need to wire up so many houses in a day. You do it for a construction company that has been contracted by a developer; and the developer wants the job done as fast as possible in order that their property can be sold and occupied as fast as possible. The professional onus is on you, the bricklayer, the carpenter, the mason, the engineer. This logic cuts across the entire board, for 'professions' as well as 'trades', which, if they haven't been entirely deskilled, are certainly getting professionally dehumanised.

Even medical doctors feel the brunt of the professionalisation of their practice, coming up against the latest demands of a changing NHS system – with increasing burdens and responsibilities, increasing scrutiny and evaluation of performance. Less time for front-line patient care and contact, more time spent in form-filling, box-ticking, and preparing for Care Quality Commission inspections.

This institutional drive is the problem. Forms of labour are often devised by professional bodies, by professional apparatuses, by professional 'experts'. It is professionalisation that annihilates the labour of love, that dowses the Hobby-Horsical flames of pure pleasure. Professionals set the terms. Employees doing the jobs have to justify themselves by delivering on the performance principle that these expert professionals have established. That's what professionalisation is. It involves professionals who don't teach setting targets on teachers; professionals who never set foot in the trenches or on the front line dictating how deep those trenches should be and what this front line is. Professionals who know nothing about actual labour processes professionalise those processes, determine the performance metrics, the outputs and the goals, their management and implementation. It's the professional performative context that rules supreme, raining terror and anxiety down on many workers and on professionals themselves.

Professionalisation, in a nutshell, is the purveyor of bad faith. It's the faith of bad faith. Professionalisation eventually leads anybody operating under its dictates to hate their job, even though they might love what they do, love the doing itself. (This was the situation I once found myself in with academia.) Somebody might feel intimately connected to the content of what they do, yet the form of this content is more and more wrenched away from the activity of the doer. The doer is alienated from the activity of labour, from their object of labour. Eventually, they're alienated from themselves – subject and object become decoupled. At that point, in order to live with yourself, bad faith impregnates you. The basis of your labour process becomes one of separation. Bad faith is a response, sometimes an understandable response, of humans coming to terms with separation, in a psychic search for reparation. As Sartre says, bad faith is 'a double activity in the heart of unity, tending on the one hand to maintain and locate the thing to be concealed and on the other hand to repress and disguise it'.[5]

This separation is an '*ism*', the professional*ism* of the job. It is equally an '*isation*', the professional*isation* of the job, of the person, of society. Separation is a source of bad faith in the individual and in their situation, to the degree that more and more people are incapacitated to perceive a world of possibilities, of alternatives that can be envisioned, struggled over, reached for and grasped. More and more people are deadened and dazed by working too hard and too long, often in jobs that mean nothing to them. Sartre calls bad faith a state of being, a 'slave to the present', shackled to a situation of existence rather than one of striving. To work in good faith is to work in the knowledge of one's freedom to choose – one's freedom to do something else, or the same thing in a different way, a different situation.

A slave to the present is a slave to the *facticity* of life, a slave to the here and now, to the what is and only is. A slave to the intractability of facts. But Sartrean existentialism, at its most upbeat moments, wants none of this. Free human beings have an obligation, Sartre says, no matter how hard it is, to try and transcend this reality of facts, to subjectify rather than objectify themselves. We have the power inside us to imagine a different world and to make it come true. Our power comes through conscious action, through active imagination – that Queen of the Faculties, as Baudelaire said. To do this is to be free, perhaps even a free professional, unencumbered by the dead weight of professionalism.

We might recognise this like a Sartrean café waiter who recognises himself playing a silly game, and decides that he needs to subvert this silly game. To cast off bad faith isn't to deny the ambiguity of one's existence but to acknowledge the double agency inherent in any situation, and that it can be subverted. To assert amateurism is to break out of the daydream world that we are entranced by, that we're contracted into; the world that won't let us slow down.

Some professionals who condition our lives, in business and in the state, are outside of us, above us, beyond our reach. They are true believers that have to be politically confronted. But other professionals are inside us, and sometimes *are us*. We are not powerless there. Professional apparatuses are constituted by professional agents; the apparatus functions only insofar as the agent plays along, only insofar as we accept our interpellation, accept our hailing, the recruitment to our station, as a compliant professional subject. Can we turn the other way when we hear that call? 'Hey, you there!' 'No, not me!' Can we look through the mirror in front of us and contest that ideological reflection? Shatter its glass and recreate for ourselves, from the shards before us, a truer identity in good faith?

In thinking about the 'truthful' self, the self that might be lurking somewhere inside, Louis Malle's 1981 film *My Dinner with André* offers some interesting help; at least, it's always offered me some kind of help. Nothing much happens in *My Dinner with André*. That's probably why it helps. It is low-budget anti-cinema, filmed by a cinematic master. There is no action, no music (apart from Satie's *Gymnopédie* No. 1 at the end), no gimmicks, just a couple of hours slowly unfolding. Two middle-aged theatre guys – Wallace (Wally) Shawn and André Gregory (the eponymous André) – talk and eat in a New York restaurant, guys playing themselves, pals who haven't seen each other for a while. But strangely, something riveting takes place. They talk theatre. They talk performance: when you are acting, when not, when onstage and when off. 'You see', André says to Wally, 'we're trying to find the truthful impulse'. The truthful impulse is 'to not do what you should do or ought to do or what is expected of you, but trying to find out what it is that you really want to do or need to do or have to do'.[6]

André, we hear, helped Wally get his first theatre break. Since then, André has opted out of the limelight, taken off on mystical adventures to Tibet and India, to deserted Polish forests. Everybody believed he'd flipped. Wally presents him as if he has flipped, cracked up. The dialogue starts off lightly, even whimsically, but the intensity and gravity get steadily ratcheted up. It is André's existential voyage that dominates; he could talk all day and night if need be. Wally, the realist and sceptic, verging on the cynic, worries more about paying his next month's rent. If he's not a slave to bad faith, he's certainly beholden to it, torn apart by it, and doesn't quite know what to do about it.

André, on the other hand, is an avant-garde amateur searching for other principles, for new meaning. His days of performing and pretending onstage – on the stage of real life – in a drama he hasn't scripted or produced, are done. He is a probing man of the anti-spectacle, bemoaning the modern world's incapacity to feel anymore, smothered as it is by electric blankets, central heating and air-conditioning, overwhelmed by quantification and professionalisation. People no longer have time to think, no longer want to think. André speaks about alienation like the young Karl Marx. At one point he even sounds like a 1960s Situationist: 'We're bored, we're all bored; we've turned into robots.' 'But has it ever occurred to you, Wally,' he challenges his friend, 'that the process which creates this boredom that we see in the world now may very well be a self-perpetuating, unconscious form of brainwashing created by a world totalitarian government based on money?' 'Somebody who is bored is asleep,' André says, 'and somebody who's asleep will not say no.'

Disillusioned with conventional theatre, André dropped out of it for years. So many people are performing so well in their every-day life, he says, that staged performance has become superfluous, even obscene. André tells Wally he is now following the radical path staked out by his close friend and guru, the Polish theatre director Jerzy Grotowski, who in the 1970s likewise abandoned conventional theatre to explore a new phase he called 'post-theatre' or 'paratheatre'.

In 1968, Grotowski published *Towards a Poor Theatre*, which immediately became an authority for avant-garde theatrical people. Grotowski never ceased asking the fundamental question: 'What is theatre?' What he calls 'Rich Theatre' – 'Professional Theatre', we might call it – lacks backbone or integrity. It's all about gran-diose sets and dazzling décor, star actors and high-tech lighting, ornate costumes and nimble changes of scenery. All of which, for Grotowski, fosters passivity rather than empathy. Worse, it's theatre masquerading as cinema, theatre's sad attempt to compete with film and television. But why bother? Why not draw on low-tech resources, on amateur resources? 'If the theatre cannot be richer than cinema,' Grotowski writes, 'then let it be *poor*. If it cannot be as lavish as television, then let it be ascetic. If it cannot be a technical attraction, let it renounce all outward technique.'[7]

Hence Poor Theatre, a theatre that does without lights, music, and scenery; a theatre that even does without theatre. It's a fascinating concept and a suggestive metaphor for life. Grotowski pushed the physical and existential limits of theatre so far that he began crossing the boundary, straying over a theoretical threshold, going beyond theatre only to enrich theatre. Pushing and prodding, he'd worked to collapse the actor-spectator gap to such a degree that now each congealed into a new theatrical subject: the participant in life. 'We noted', Grotowski says, 'that when we eliminate certain blocks and obstacles what remains is what is most elementary and most simple – what exists between human beings when they have a certain confidence between each other and when they look for an understanding that goes beyond the understanding of words ... Precisely at that point one does not perform anymore.'

Throughout the 1970s, the setting for Grotowski's 'Laboratorium' projects was a retreat thirty miles outside the Polish town of Wroclaw. Some of the most noted personalities from experimental theatre – André Gregory included – undertook pilgrimages to the Laboratorium. Nearly every evening, a key element in paratheatrics unfolded, the so-called Beehive: a collective improvisation of elemental experiences, open to all comers, always led by the participants themselves. Gregory describes these encounters as a 'great human kaleidoscope', an evening made up of 'shiftings of the kaleidoscope'. Beehives lasted four or five hours, winding down in the early hours of the morning, at daybreak.

Instead of playing a role, André tells Wally, a character in, say, a Chekhov set piece, instead of acting on behalf of that fictional character, in the Beehive you yourself become the character. Now, 'you have no imaginary situation to hide behind, and you have no other person to hide behind.' And the theme or the plot is made up of who 'we' all are together. The question becomes how to bring to action this theme – how to find the theme through action, and how action is created by impulse. 'In a way', says André, 'it's going right back to childhood, where simply a group of children enter a room or are brought into a room, without toys, and they begin to play. Grown-ups were learning how to play again.'

What is happening here, André thinks, is something to do with living. 'I think I experienced for the first time', he tells Wally, 'what it means to be truly alive.' What was amazing about these workshops 'was how quickly people seemed to fall into enthusiasm, celebration, joy, wonder, abandon, wildness, tenderness. And could we stand to live like that? I mean, maybe we're just simply afraid of living?'

These encounters create situations in which people follow the 'laws of theatrical improvisation' – do whatever their impulse as the character prompts them to do – except that in this improvisation, the theme is oneself: the character is *you*. With no imaginary situation to hide behind, no other person to hide behind, no more bad faith to paralyse you. 'What you're doing, in fact', says André, is going back to Stanislavsky's system, 'asking those questions any actor should ask themselves as a character – Who am I? Why am I here? Where do I come from? And where am I going? – but instead of applying them to a role, you apply them to yourself.' You no longer 'play the part' or inhabit the role; you become the character in the life performance.

The problem is that we are not looking, not thinking, not asking ourselves anything. We are being too easy on ourselves. We are walking around in some kind of fog, in a trance, like zombies. 'I mean, I don't think we're even aware of ourselves or of our own reaction to things', so habitual has the automation become, so deeply is our consciousness impregnated with professional performative ideology, the rituals of mindless, senseless repetition. 'We're all too busy performing.' 'And so everyone acts as if they know exactly how they ought to conduct themselves at every single moment, and they all seem totally self-confident.'

'Even though', Wally says, interrupting André,

> by performing these roles all the time we're hiding the reality of ourselves from everyone else … The incredible emphasis we place now on our so-called careers automatically makes perceiving reality a very low priority, because if your life is organised around trying to be successful in a career, then it doesn't matter what you perceive or what you experience. You're just thinking, well, have I done the thing that I planned? Have I performed this necessary action for my career? And so you really can sort of shut your mind off for years ahead in a way. You can sort of turn on the automatic pilot.

Life becomes habitual. On goes the autopilot. 'And if you're just operating by habit,' agrees André,

> then you're not really living. I mean, you know, in Sanskrit, the root verb 'to be' is the same as 'to grow' or to 'make grow' … The trouble with always being active and doing things is that it's quite possible to do all sorts of things and at the same time be completely dead inside. You're doing all these things, but are you doing them because you really feel an impulse to do them, or are you doing them mechanically … Because I do believe that if you're just living mechanically, then you have to change your life.

'I think there comes a time when you need to do that', André says at the end of *My Dinner with André*. The restaurant has emptied out; all the other customers seem to have left hours ago; Satie starts to play. 'You need to cut out the noise.'

As people's lives become dominated by professionalism and professionalisation, other recalcitrant spirits will appear. They will try to construct a new future for the world, invent 'new pockets of light'. They will resist by creating what André calls 'a new kind of school or a new kind of monastery', a new kind of 'reserve'. This reserve, he says, will be an island of safety where history is remembered and human beings continue to function. We are talking about an 'underground', he says, 'which did exist during the Dark Ages in a different way … And the purpose of this underground is to find out how to preserve the culture. How to keep things living.'

Still, the route to authenticity, we know, won't be through opting out; remember Dave Eggers's *The Circle*, how Mercer tried that to his detriment? Good faith will have to push beyond Hegel: it will have to look the negative in the face and move through it, within it, like Baudelaire did with modernity, not run away from it. I think Guillaume Paoli got it right when he said that the ultimate limits of contemporary capitalism aren't geographical, aren't objective, aren't about its upper technical and economic reach; that they aren't 'natural' limits.

They're subjective limits, limits inside us, here for us to resist, to block and overturn, to redirect. We can put up barriers to this system from within, prevent the continued fracking of human value, stop kneeling down before its professional altar, uttering its expert prayers, performing on its payroll – having it represent us. At the same time, existential literature is correct to insist on the need for us to transcend this state of affairs, to transcend ourselves, to participate in our own lives as we remake our political culture.

Participation in the creation of your own life hinges on your participation in political life. The two go together: you might not be interested in politics, but politics is always going to be interested in you. At the end of his debut book, *The Politics of Authenticity*, Marshall Berman argued against dropping out, against fleeing to some velvet underground, to some reserve or island of safety. He would have sympathetically disagreed with André's opinions about escape. Of course, when good faith seems so far off, the self might survive in the near term through dropping out, giving back its entrance ticket to the professional rat race.[8] But that will only ever be a hollow victory: 'totalitarian society would welcome this project of dropping out,' Marshall says, 'which could get its most authentic and hence most dangerous citizens freely and quietly out of the way.'[9]

This is another way of saying that 'amateur identities' are secured only through 'amateur politics' – maybe even through an 'amateur revolution'. Yet amateur politics, in turn, can only be achieved through amateur identities asserting their collective amateurism, enacting their personal and civic allegiance to some passionate project. Amateur politics and amateur identities fuel and sustain one another. They do so for a good reason: amateur personalities will be vulnerable identities forever up against the professional machine. They will be minor characters who will need other minor characters for support and solidarity, in order to grow strong. Together they might make something amateurishly affirmative, enabling them to live beyond the negative, beyond the state of demotivation and disaffection. Can everyone affirm their Hobby-Horse and not only earn a living but organise a society? I'm not sure. Hypothetically, I like to think yes. But what I'd love to see is a movement pushing towards a stage where we can test out this hypothesis empirically.

In the meantime, it's evident that many jobs are dead zones designed to perpetuate the ideology of work. I'd almost go so far as saying that work is a ruling-class conspiracy, a conspiracy of professionals, cooked up to keep people off the streets and out of mischief. People do jobs so meaningless that it is redundant labour even when you are actively in work. These are jobs nobody would ever miss. The same could be said of highly paid jobs in finance and real estate: society would be better off without them. So why not eliminate them, as well as the institutions that legitimise these jobs? One of the greatest releases of amateur vital powers would be a society that did away with purposeless work, that removed the intricate divisions of labour which force professionals and non-professionals alike to function as mere appendages of machines, on assembly lines and at check-out tills, in front of computer terminals and laptops – longer and longer, faster and faster.

True amateurism thrives in the realm of freedom rather than in that of necessity. A society of good faith would not so much abolish divisions of labour as neutralise them, socialise them, periodically switching tasks around to enable people to vary their activities, let individuals identify with their activity. Even menial jobs like emptying bins could bring real satisfaction if the demon workload didn't weigh too heavily and if the social benefits could be more directly felt. Most important would be to mitigate the intensity and flow of any uniform activity, translating productive gains from technology into job sharing and increased free time. Socially necessary labour time would take on a new, rebooted meaning.

If there's one great message to retain from Marx, it's that he regarded *time* as our most precious asset, the wellspring of potential social and personal riches, of real human capital. Time is something too important to let slip away unfulfilled. The good use of free time is crucial for full human individuality, for any expressive amateurism, for self-unfolding, for expanding individual capacities to discover Hobby-Horsical matters. It's a recipe for the creation and perpetuation of a better society, with happier people. A society where time has been liberated and where people have disposable time on their hands, is a society in which one's 'second life' (as Marx calls it) outside the workplace becomes one's 'real life'.

As we strive towards that point, the power of amateurs to think critically and live passionately is not a power summoned up to run away from contradictions; it is the power needed to confront contradictions, within the self as well as in society. People need to enter into their respective flow as a contraflow. It is the power to see into ourselves, to see through the disguises a professionalised system has made us wear. I am still inspired by Edward Said's notion of amateurism, that voice I heard so long ago, insisting we reconnect to more meaningful, personal projects, to more original thoughts. Are we here to be bought off, pacified and numbed? Or are we here to challenge and provoke, to stir ourselves into opposition, into collective, democratic action?

These are questions we might want to heed, whether or not we function as intellectuals or have the capacity to intellectualise. To be an amateur is to perform for yourself, to draft the script to your own life, and ideally to do it with others. It is to be self-employed in life, not simply in work, a state of Being as well as a mode of doing. It is to do things well because you're intimately connected to what you do, because doing well correlates positively with being well, with well-being. To be an amateur is to enrich yourself beyond wealth. Amateurism is an affair of the heart, like love. It is complicated and messy, often tumultuous. But it is always about honest human expression.

9

The Amateur Revolution

Amateur politics is the antithesis of professional democracy. It is a practice that helps release amateur identities, lets them flow out, lifting the lid on established politics. By amateur politics I mean one that flies under the institutional radar, a politics that involves the participation of smart, non-specialised people. Amateur politics will likely be 'unofficial', at least to begin with; it will take place outside the party political structure, outside parliamentarianism, outside professional agencies, maybe even outside the law.

It usually develops on the margins before it advances into the core. It might be trivial or significant. Of course, it's impossible to predict whether a trivial amateur politics will one day become significant, or if the significant will eventually get trivialised. Significant amateur politics might start out trivial and yet generate momentum in unexpected ways, with unforeseeable results and surprising outcomes, maybe even revolutionary outcomes, all of which somehow *last*. The small sometimes leads to the big; the big invariably begins small.

Big participation might mean citizen participation, ordinary people getting involved in a bigger campaign, in a social movement, demanding something they don't have or contesting something they don't want. Small participation might mean individual acts of subversion, direct and indirect, explicit and covert, done, say, at work, via a demotivation here, a slowdown there; or in public spaces, like Rosa Parks circa 1955, sitting on the 'vanilla' rather than the 'chocolate' side of the bus in Birmingham, Alabama. A small gesture of defiance that led to a bigger politics, to a bigger feat of participation, helping kick-start a whole civil rights movement. Minor characters become major protagonists, vital activists in social transformations that are occasionally revolutionary.

Lenin, the great Russian revolutionary, put a different spin on the concept of 'professionalism', insisting that revolutionary politics need *professional* revolutionaries. He sometimes sounds a lot like Plato: the revolution, Lenin says in *What Is to Be Done?* (1902), needs 'wise men'. By wise men, 'I mean *professional revolutionaries.*' 'We must have a committee of professional *revolutionaries* ... We professional revolutionaries must and will make it our business to engage in this kind of "pushing on" a hundred times more forcibly than we have done hitherto.'[1] True, Lenin's professionalism led to the fulfilment of a collective revolutionary dream, guided by an apparently selfless humanitarian. But it equally became the most savage indictment of what professional politics sometimes entailed: pragmatic ruthlessness, implemented by politicians devoid of any kind of human feeling, of anything personal, of any love or fear.

In *To the Finland Station*, Edmund Wilson tells how Lenin avoided listening to the Beethoven he loved: he feared the wonderful music would move him, make him soft, inspire him to drop his steely guard. 'I know nothing greater than [Beethoven's] *Appassionata*', Wilson quotes Lenin as saying. 'I'd like to listen to it every day. It is marvellous, superhuman music.' Wilson continues: 'Then, screwing up his eyes and smiling, Lenin added, rather sadly: "But I can't listen to music too often. It affects your nerves, makes you want to say stupid nice things and stroke the heads of people ... And now you mustn't stroke anyone's head – you might get your hand bitten off. You have to hit them on the head, without mercy ... Our duty is infernally hard."[2]

Somebody who had problems with this line was Hannah Arendt. Maybe it's no coincidence: Arendt wasn't a 'wise man' but a 'wise woman', another amateur in fact. She was a trained philosopher, a former student of Martin Heidegger and Karl Jaspers; yet as an émigré Jew who fled her native Germany in the 1940s, she reinvented herself in Anglophone New York. She learned to write, painstakingly, in English, and penned detailed thought-pieces for non-specialist audiences – introducing Walter Benjamin to America and reporting from Jerusalem on the Adolf Eichmann trial, both for the *New Yorker*.[3] Arendt championed big, heterodox ideas, strayed across disciplines and was an irreverent independent after Edward Said's own heart, an outspoken thinker, a public intellectual always in exile. She never lost a feeling of 'distance' from the English language, she said, nor did she ever see political theory as any kind of 'profession'.[4]

In *On Revolution*, published in 1963, Arendt is critical of Lenin's revolutionary paradigm. In response, she unearths the *amateur revolution*. Amateurs didn't only organise the city in times of revolutionary upheaval, Arendt said, like in the 1871 Paris Commune; amateurs were also the principal instigators. Amateurs in revolt literally *made* the revolution, and, who knows, may still make the revolution again. Close examination of revolutionary history reveals how amateurs were behind what Arendt calls the 'lost treasures of the revolutionary tradition': the popular councils, those spontaneously cohering organs that were made up of ordinary people, run by ordinary people, outside of revolutionary parties.

Such councils were entirely unexpected by revolutionary parties and their leaders.

Arendt's point is a populist one: no professional, not even a *professional revolutionary*, made or will ever make the revolution. No past revolution, she says, can be attributed to professional revolutionaries. Usually it was the other way around: 'revolution broke out and liberated, as it were, the professional revolutionists from wherever they happened to be – from jail, or from the coffee house, or from the library. Not even Lenin's party of professional revolutionists would ever have been able to "make" a revolution; the best they could do was to be around, or to hurry home, at the right moment, at the moment of collapse.'[5]

In *On Revolution*, Arendt seldom mentions Rosa Luxemburg, the tragic Polish Marxist. But she and Arendt were kindred spirits in their distrust of Lenin's 'ultra-centralist tendency'. Both women rejected Lenin's contempt for non-aligned working-class activism in favour of the 'objectivity' of a professional Party elite. Different progressive and working-class federations, Luxemburg wrote in *The Russian Revolution, and Leninism or Marxism?* (1918), needed a 'liberty of action'. That way they could better 'develop their revolutionary initiative and … utilise all the resources of a situation'. Lenin's line was 'full of the sterile spirit of the overseer. It is not a positive and creative spirit.' Like Arendt, Luxemburg is more generous, more sensitive to the ups and downs of struggle, in the course of which an organisation emanates and grows, unpredictably pell-mell. Social democracy, Luxemburg said, isn't just 'invented'; it is 'the product of a series of great creative acts of the often spontaneous class struggle seeking its way forward'.

Arendt agrees. She points out that the councils' chief characteristic is the spontaneity of their emergence. They flagrantly contradict the twentieth century's model of revolution, 'planned, prepared, and executed almost to cold scientific exactness by professional revolutionists'. The councils were administered by amateurs, by inexperienced yet passionate people who, in their spare time, created a communal culture and society at a moment of revolutionary tumult.

They became paragons of political amateurism, of the romantic yearnings of a popular collective rich in feeling, unashamedly hopeful and warm. It's a definition I like, even if it sounds naïve in professional times. With non-specialists at the helm and professionals kept at bay, the horizon of empathy expands. People might screw things up along the way; but it's a more inclusive way to learn together, to turn the small into something bigger, to discover democracy, rather than have it custom-built and shoved in your face.

Hannah Arendt had a couple of contemporaries who might have agreed, women both: Jane Jacobs and Rachel Carson. Each wrote bestselling books within a year of one another: *Death and Life of Great American Cities* (1961) and *Silent Spring* (1962). As 'housewives' with no institutional affiliation, Jacobs, a trained journalist, and Carson, a qualified marine biologist, were frequently dismissed in equal measure as rank amateurs with a poor handle on their subjects, not like professional planners and scientists. *Time* magazine laid into Carson for her 'emotion-fanning words'; she was 'unfair and one-sided', they said, 'hysterically overemphatic'. It's no surprise that much amateur politics has been carried out by women. And it's no surprise either that this politics grounds itself in ordinary everyday life. Jacobs and Carson were at home, saw things close up, were responsible for the school run and the daily shopping. Carson, when she wasn't writing or campaigning, looked after her mother and cared for her adopted son, despite having terminal breast cancer.

Like many other more unsung amateurs, Jacobs and Carson stood up to professionals, held their passionate ground and altered the course of history in small yet significant ways. Jacobs helped inspire community activism, a central plank of radicalism that defined 'the Sixties'; Carson was the godmother of a grass-roots environmental movement that really took off in the 1970s. Both called into question the principle of 'scientific' progress that underpinned post-war American culture and now underpins twenty-first-century culture everywhere.

Carson's and Jacobs's amateur politics revolved around activities we might label 'reproductive' rather than productive; they were home-baked rather than work-based. Each saw how the reproduction of the countryside and the reproduction of urban life were endangered, threatened by similar professional forces engaged in the same, depersonalised, professional business of destruction. In Carson's case, it was the pharmaceutical companies with their DDT pesticides, killing birds and insects, polluting rivers. Toxic DDT was spraying the Vietcong in the South-East Asian bush; in rural America, too, Carson said, it was a lethal agent dowsing forests and farmland.

One of Carson's most enduring metaphors is 'The Other Road'. 'We stand now', she said, 'where two roads diverge. They are not equally fair. The road we have long been traveling is deceptively easy, a smooth superhighway on which we progress with great speed, but at its end lies disaster. The other fork of the road – the one "less traveled by" – offers our last, our only chance to reach a destination that assures the preservation of our earth.'[6] The choice is ours to make, she says. But in helping us make that choice, 'we should no longer accept the counsel of those who tell us that we must fill our world with poisonous chemicals: we should look about and see what other course is open to us.'

Carson's, like Jacobs's, was a one-woman campaign that soon became part of a larger collective movement of awareness and revolt. This gathered momentum throughout the 1960s, concerning itself not only with the all-too-comfy ties between professional scientists and the chemical business, but also with the threat of nuclear war and radiation contamination, animal welfare, the dumping of hazardous wastes in the oceans – one of Carson's earlier books was *The Sea Around Us* – and what Carson called 'the right to know', publicly announcing a marked distrust of those specialists on the commercial payroll. Carson was stressing the interconnectedness of the human and natural world, the relationship of an undersea to an oversea. She questioned the whole attitude of industrial society towards the natural world. Her 'fable of tomorrow' is our world today.

This idea of 'two roads' was equally prominent in Jane Jacobs's political lexicon. One road – the professional route – had now turned into the mighty expressway that was decimating the less travelled back streets and street-corner societies so precious to Jacobs. Planners, architects, property developers and bureaucrats hell-bent on profitable rational destruction, packaged as urban renewal, were letting the expressways hurtle through built-up America. They seemed engaged in a guerrilla war against urban America itself, seeing off whole neighbourhoods up and down the country, destroying economic and cultural vitality. The specialists likewise denounced Jacobs's great book about great cities. She wrote it without any credentials, they said, without formal architectural or planning training, without even a university degree. And yet, precisely because of that, it voiced a refreshing counter-narrative on the page, while acting out this narrative in the street. Jacobs's brilliance, like Carson's, wasn't only her vision but also the timing of this vision, the enactment of it, and the mood she set with it.

Hers was a defiance of professional hubris, especially the male professional hubris of tyrants like the developer Robert Moses. Jacobs's 'lost' tradition of the city resembles Arendt's 'lost' tradition of revolution. The latter pinpointed the spontaneously erupting neighbourhood councils; the former pointed out that 'the kind of planning for a city that really works would be a sort of informed, intelligent improvisation.'[7] Arendt's grumble about professional politics was like a leaf out of Jacobs's own book: 'The trouble lies in the lack of public spaces to which people at large would have entrance ... The trouble, in other words, is that politics has become a profession and a career, and that the "elite" therefore is being chosen according to standards and criteria which are themselves profoundly unpolitical.'[8]

When Robert Moses planned to plough a huge swath through lower Manhattan to build yet another giant road, the multi-storey Lower Manhattan Expressway, razing many vibrant communities in Greenwich Village and SoHo in the process, Jacobs and her fellow residents mobilised to 'KILL THE XPRESSWAY NOW!' She was arrested for inciting a riot. But Jacobs knew how to defend herself, how to organise, how to get publicity, how to mobilise the troops, how to form coalitions with other amateurs. At one public hearing, Moses decried his antagonists: 'There's nobody against this – *nobody, nobody, nobody*, but a bunch of, a bunch of mothers!' And he stomped out. Jacobs's genius was showing how amateurs could band together to create a popular power few could have imagined beforehand, herself included.

At a hearing at the New York City Board of Estimate, Jacobs and fellow citizens ventured across the stage to get an audience with the bigwig professionals sat above. 'And this threw them into the most incredible tizzy', she recalls, 'the idea of unarmed, perfectly gentle human beings just coming up and getting in close contact with them. You never saw people so frightened.' Here were citizens who hitherto didn't know one another, who were blind to one another, who perhaps even disliked one another, coming together because they, as ordinary amateurs, wanted to challenge the professional development flow. Weakness binds people together, making weakness strength. The formula was simple, but it still inspires. Jacobs summed it up a few years before her death (in 2006), in an interview on Canadian TV: '*Responsible people oppose absurd ideas.*'

In a curious way, I glimpsed this myself, not so long ago, in the wreckage of Athens, in Greece, happening almost behind the backs of Athenians as they struggle with the crisis amidst a Eurozone meltdown. When all is gone, all is seemingly lost, there's nothing left but each other. Out of this nothingness something beautiful can be created, something full. I glimpsed this fullness in the solidarity and warmth expressed by a cohort of young Greek women activist-researchers, who, since 2010, have called themselves 'Encounter Athens'.

Encounter Athens have been vocal in trying to resurrect critical debate around public affairs in Athens. They've organised and spoken out at workshops and demonstrations about such topics as the mainstream media's inciting of a politics of fear, the rising xenophobic violence, and the lack of affordable housing in the city. They've been mobilising people against the auctioning off of Greek cultural heritage by the Hellenic Republic Asset Development Fund (TAIPED). A purported fiscal strategy, TAIPED is a privatisation scam, imposed in 2011 by Troika professionals and rubber-stamped by Greece's then centre-right government.

The Fund isn't so much a public entity as a lucrative private portfolio, a 'limited liability company' with the explicit goal of

selling state-owned assets – land, infrastructure, public companies, airports (e.g. Hellinikon Airport), coastal fronts, even
whole islands – to repay the nation's debt. Yet once sold off, these
assets can't be transferred back to the state: they remain in private
hands, enshrined in private law. TAIPED grants 'investment
incentives' that blithely ignore statutory land-use and environmental regulation. It is a vehicle for a massive land-grab, a fire sale
of state-owned property vital to both present and future Greek
society, merely to repay a debt that is commonly acknowledged to
be unsustainable. A massive bargain-basement asset clearance is
under way, exchanging Greece's long-range future for immediate
liquidity to satisfy the Troika's fantasy fiscal targets.

I'd met Encounter Athens in Exarcheia, a grungy neighbourhood with anarchist leanings, sitting outside in the balmy May
night air in one of its many bars, a stone's throw away from
Navarinou Park. For years, the park had languished as a makeshift
parking lot; but in 2009, local anarchists reclaimed it. They put in
considerable amateur sweat equity to transform drab concrete into
an exotic green oasis, an experimental community garden. Fruit
and vegetables are grown; local residents reconnect to the land;
kids play free of cars. The park acts as an ad hoc cultural space,
too, a place for hanging out and lingering; movies get projected,
and, like the evening I was there, musicians groove. From the
bar we could hear partying. Revellers were commemorating the
park's fifth anniversary, or, one might say, feting micro-militancy
as non-monetised urban sustainability.

Despite the nearby celebrations, the Encounter Athens women
were subdued, depressed at the personal and political state of
affairs. They're hanging on, but only just, they told me. They're
tired, feeling like they're fighting a losing battle. 'What should
we do?' they asked me. 'Keep going, keep battling', I said lamely,

somewhat embarrassed, because it sounded so banal and facile. I'd have loved to produce an easy answer, an absolute practical answer, a *What Is to Be Done* answer, but there is none; I knew it, they knew it. Our conversations were deeply political, deeply engaged and engaging. They told me they had no money anymore. They're writing up PhDs but know that afterwards there'll be no jobs, certainly no academic jobs, not in their working lifetimes. They can't afford to buy clothes or shoes. Some have been forced to move back with their parents, who themselves hustle to live off dwindling pensions and benefits.

As we left in the early hours, everywhere in Exarcheia was deserted. In the darkness, it suddenly struck me that inside all this negativity, deep within it, lay an amazing positivity, a wonderful source of inspiration about how to live differently. I didn't want to romanticise hardship, but I'd witnessed a mode of living that dispensed with *representation*: with money as a representation of value, with mass media as a representation of truth, with professional government as a vehicle for democracy. All that had been stripped away to leave a bare, unaccommodated life, a life directly lived, without mediation.

The women from Encounter Athens had other concerns than the stuff young men and women interest themselves in elsewhere, like fashion and conventional ambition, making money and owning property (and being mortgaged to the hilt), doing a job (usually a not very interesting job) and slavishly following a banal capitalist image of success. The billboards around Athens stand empty: there's no point advertising to a populace without money, to people whose life is no longer defined by conspicuous consumption. There's something else at stake now, something else worth fighting for: a life with common, intangible assets, a shared public life. A new, Millennial generation is emerging, a coming community, defined by young people feverishly discussing politics and reinventing the notion of the Greek agora, even if they don't know it yet. That's how they occupy their time: with politics. They're going forwards by reverting to their ancient tradition, coming of age as *political animals*—which is what Plato meant all along by natural human existence.

I'd witnessed something similar in Sweden, too, where there were glimmers of hope from its youth, even if this hope always entered through the back door, clandestinely. The once-feted egalitarian, social democratic Swedish model is steadily getting dismantled, privatised and sold off. Private companies now cash in on tax-payers' land and tax-funded schools; the housing market has been deregulated; gentrification is rife. The country has an income gap widening faster than even Britain's; there's a particularly glaring gulf between native Swedes and foreign-born workers.

In 2013, Stockholm's *banlieue*, Husby, revolted, went up in flames. Police clashed with immigrants in Malmö as well. These urban explosions are a dissent that liberal-bourgeois institutions can't handle, can't accommodate. The people on the streets lobbing Molotov cocktails or burning cars, looting stores or protesting peacefully, are younger folk excluded from the professional decision-making process, denied the trappings of the privatised good life. What's been happening in Sweden, as elsewhere, is a political as well as institutional failing, a failing of professional democracy, a failing of neoliberal bourgeois society; it has little to do with wanton criminality.

A coming community is being nurtured in Möllevången, a long-standing working-class district in Malmö, once on the city limits. In the heart of the neighbourhood is the Amalthea radical book-store, a small autonomous space run by a loose cohort of amateur volunteers – students, ex-students, unemployed, young 'professionals' – who thirst for radical ideas. They manage the small anarchist, Marxist and feminist stock and tend a tiny café. They conduct lectures, readings and teach-ins, all without any formal organisation.

The bookstore was named after a bombing incident in 1908: the *Amalthea* was a ship arriving from the UK, full of scab workers to replace Malmö's striking dockers. Three strikers rowed out in a small boat and one, Anton Nilson, a militant unionist, planted a bomb on board, killing a scab and injuring twenty-three more. Police arrested the bombers and sentenced Nilson to death. The bombing was universally condemned; but protests and public sympathy also spoke up for Nilson, whose death sentence was commuted to forced labour, along with his pals.

The Amalthea collective commemorates Nilson and the Swedish workers' movement. Anybody can become a member by attending weekly meetings and being ready to do the dishes, stack the shelves, operate the till, discuss politics and disseminate progressive ideas. Amalthea keeps the red flag flying in Malmö; and even if it is waved by relatively few people, it's important not to get too wrapped up in numbers, converting vital human ingenuity and struggle into a positivist counting exercise, as though something is only significant when lots of people take part.

Amateur politics is usually about being a *minority* anyway, about minorities finding other like-minded minorities. It's about being subversive and imaginative, and using your subversive imagination to create great things. Young people who come to Amalthea worry about things like the rise of the far right; they also worry about the future, or no future, about having no jobs, or jobs they don't want. Jobs bereft of meaning, or jobs with too much meaning, a meaning they have no way of accessing, of participating in. But by looking this negative in the face, they are already groping for answers, ensuring there will be a future, that *they* are going to help make that future.

Activism here, like in Athens, like in thousands of localities across the globe, follows in the long lineage of Jane Jacobs, even if those involved don't know it. Some do know it. Collectively, they all seem to be affirming what another savvy urbanist, Henri Lefebvre, called the 'right to the city', an expression of amateurs trying to orchestrate participatory democracy. Participation here lets people try to shape their own destinies, tries to convert passive acquiescence into active condemnation, into a positive re-appropriation culminating in the creation of something new and different. Participation dramatises social life, dramatises a potentially active citizenship. Its presence brings places to life; its absence usually denotes a place's death, because something essential is missing.

Forever the great democrat, Lefebvre, born in 1901, was likewise something of an amateur. He drank wine with Surrealist poets in the 1930s, fought with the Resistance in the 1940s, drove a cab in Paris in the 1950s, and taught sociology and philosophy at various French universities in the 1960s, when he befriended Debord and the Situationists. He was one of the intellectual godfathers of the 1968 generation. He authored sixty-odd books, introduced a whole body of Hegelian Marxism into France, and wrote prolifically about urbanism, everyday life, literature and space. Lefebvre didn't even get his first steady academic job until 1966, at the age of sixty-five! By 1973 he'd 'retired', only to embark on a world tour, writing and speaking, trying to understand an urbanisation of the future in Asia and Latin America, and in Los Angeles, a city that both fascinated and appalled him.

Lefebvre was a man of the margins, of the periphery. 'I've tried my hand in many different domains', he admitted in the 1970s. 'In this sense, I'm a non-specialist, and maintain, with a lot of pride and not without difficulty, this qualification. I say not without difficulty because many times during conferences and colloquiums, in the capacity of an academic, I find myself confronted by people who ask me: "In what field are you a specialist?" I respond, "In nothing, monsieur." These lofty souls usually then turn their backs on me.'[9]

Lefebvre's 'right to the city' is an ideal conceived from the periphery. It aims to empower outsiders to get inside. Sometimes, even, to get inside themselves. It might seem a fuzzy sort of human right. But actually, it is very concrete. It means the right to live out the city as one's own, to live *for* the city, to be happy (or unhappy) there. The right to affordable housing, a decent school for the kids, accessible services, reliable public transport. The right to have your urban horizon as wide or as narrow as you want; an allegiance to the neighbourhood, to your street and building, but also to what lies beyond.

The urban as a whole should be yours, yours to move in, yours to explore, possess, *feel* you have a stake in – should you want it. Thus, to participate doesn't necessarily mean to be engaged in politics every evening, knocking on doors and going to meetings; it can equally mean a sense of belonging to the urban realm, having a say in its well-being. It means that you feel some sense of collective, shared purpose, that you're not alienated from the city's affairs.

In the 1960s, Lefebvre linked the right to the city with a 'right to centrality'. Back then, he meant a *geographical* right to occupy the centre of the city, a city that was overpriced for ordinary dwellers, becoming gentrified and turned into a tourist spectacle (like in Paris). In the United States, the opposite pattern prevailed:

the centre then was being abandoned. Richer, white populations were fleeing inner cities in favour of the burgeoning suburbs; the tattered shards of the urban core were left largely to the most marginalised, to minority populations, to the most geographically immobile. The latter's right to centrality never meant much until a Back-to-the-City movement began to economically colonise the inner cities again in the 1990s, forcing many poorer people out.

Today, if we were to creatively reframe the 'right to centrality', we would see it less as a geographical right than as an *existential* and *political* right. The right to centrality expresses a desire to make yourself the centre of your own life, the centre of your own developmental process; to make your neighbourhood a liveable neighbourhood. And if that neighbourhood is on the periphery, then the right to centrality means that the periphery should be the centre of your Being.

In any case, the future for the bulk of the world's urban populations lies beyond notions of centre. It is constituted by a sprawling urbanism without a centre, at least without a clearly defined geographical centre. The right to the city is the right to stay put, to reside where you are, to afford to reside where you are, to be able to make it your own. It's your right to be centred wherever you want to exist, any place you want to call home. To fight for your source of comfort when the outside world betrays you.

Hannah Arendt brilliantly expressed this same impulse in the late 1950s:

The *polis*, properly speaking, is not the city-state in its physical location; it is the organisation of the people as it arises out of acting and speaking together, and its true space lies between people living together for this purpose, no matter where they happen to be. 'Wherever you go will be a *polis*': these famous Greek words … expressed the conviction that action and speech create a space between participants which can find its proper location almost any time and anywhere.[10]

'The city-state', Arendt said, 'must be considered to be "humans writ large".'

In the 1980s, Lefebvre was more adamant than ever that professional institutions were the enemy of a participatory urban life. A new state model, he said, was imposing itself, under whose writ municipalities would soon be finally subsumed. (Bourdieu would agree.) Lefebvre could never have imagined the true depth and breadth of this new state model, or guessed what was in store during the two decades following his death (in 1991). But he was prescient: professional democracy reproduces its own customs of management and domination. It's no exaggeration to say that the formal rights of citizens continue to be reduced, along with the scope to exercise those rights. A fresh vision is required, Lefebvre said, a new sort of citizenship and belonging. By 1989, he claimed that 'the right to the city implies nothing less than a revolutionary conception of citizenship.'[11]

This citizenship has little to do with passports. It's a citizenship that lies inside and beyond any passport we can traditionally recognise, the kind rubber-stamped by an official institution of a nation-state. It's a citizenship involving another sort of passport, a more spectral and clandestine one, expressive of a citizenry waiting in the wings, yet to assert itself, yet to fly its flag. Let's call this passport a *shadow passport*, the identity document and travel permit of a *shadow citizenry*.

Today's shadow citizenry haunts its Other, its shadow ruling class, the unaccountable agents who we've seen pulling the strings of professional democracy and who call the shots pretty much everywhere. To be the bearer of a shadow passport is to express a latent or potential solidarity with other citizens the world over, with other disenfranchised amateur citizens. This shadow citizenry doesn't know one another, but they identify with one another. They speak different tongues, yet share collective hopes and mutual affinities; they have a similar 'structure of feeling', a feeling of being on the receiving end of somebody else's doing, frequently a powerful person's doing, a professional person's doing.

The shadow citizenry is a territorial reserve army of foot soldiers, a relative surplus population of ordinary people who want in but are forced out. They're defiant yet disunited, disgruntled and raging in a global civil war of austerity and high-frequency piracy. Shadow citizens exist in the realm where social exclusion meets spatial marginality. We might deem this shadow citizenry a family of odd ones out, people passed over, laid off, dispossessed, pushed out, rejected and exploited; and they're underground people, too, from the pages of Dostoevsky, who refuse to be victimised, overflow with rancour, and who want to challenge the structures of power that try to walk over them.

A lot of shadow citizens are undocumented migrants, refugees rejected and rebuked, profiled and patrolled no matter where they wander. Shadow citizens are a minority that's increasingly a majority: if anything, shadow citizens are the new norm, the new global default position. They're the periphery in the core, the core of the periphery. So many people have been pushed off-limits that it's extended the limit of limits, created an even larger social space for the concept of citizenship, for a new citizenship yet to be made sovereign.

Perhaps it's not too difficult to conceive the shadow citizenry today comprising a disenfranchised constituency haunting the global *banlieue*. Shadow citizens are phantoms of the periphery who feel the periphery inside them, who identify with the periphery, even if they live at the core. They encompass the NINJA generation of No Income, No Jobs, No Assets, the 15-M *indignados* on the streets of Spain, and the Occupiers denouncing unearned plenty and growing wealth inequality. And the Greeks who feel the brunt of the right-hand accountancy of European Central Bankers, IMF bureaucrats and European Commission technocrats.

Of course, there are quite a few Greeks cheering for the fascist Golden Dawn, just as there are many more clinging on for dear life to their 'official' passports, invoking ultra-nationalist purity and neo-Nazi necessity; but shadow passport holders embrace a very different kind of citizenship. They've more in common with dispossessed Arab and African youth in French suburbs, with *sans-papiers* and stateless refugees, with Palestinians lobbing rocks at Israeli tanks, with Kobane Kurds, with Detroiters beholden to 'Emergency Managers', with 'June Days' Brazilians protesting public transport hikes, with looters in London and Stockholm, with occupiers in Istanbul's Gezi Park and kids in Hong Kong's Occupy Central, with anybody and everybody who has had their home repossessed, who has defaulted on a loan, who is debt-encumbered and whose pension is, like their future, *kaput*.

Shadow citizens are also the anonymous hacktivists haunting cyberspace, the Kalden-like double agents and great refusers, the underground men and women everywhere, the Happy Unemployed, maybe even the crowds at the latest new way of doing politics, *La Nuit Debout* – standing upright most of the night in Paris's Place de la République and then coming back next morning. *Les nuitards* are a motley array of disaffected French men and women, mainly young but some old, too, wanting 'the world or nothing' (*le monde ou rien*). They bring the spirit of Occupy Wall Street to the French capital.

The shadow citizenry expresses that turbulent spirit we've come to recognise in Russian literature. The shadow passport is a major motif in Andrei Bely's revolutionary masterpiece, *Petersburg*, written in the early 1910s and set during the run-up to the aborted 1905 revolution, a decade or so before the Bolsheviks' eventual triumph. Everyone knew then that the times were changing, that politics and intrigue wafted in the air, that 'momentous events were rumbling' and something was about to give, quite soon. The story, like our own today, has 'everyone waiting for something, fearing something, hoping for something; at the slightest noise, they poured quickly on to the streets, gathered into a crowd and again dispersed.'[12] 'The shadow passport', Bely says, 'is made out inside you. You will sign it yourself by means of some extravagant little action. The little action will come to you: you will perform it yourself; that kind of signing is acknowledged amongst us as the best kind.'

In Bely's spectral realm of political intrigue, the phantom invisible stalks the official visible. 'Your complaints addressed to the visible world', we hear, 'will remain without result, like all complaints. The tragedy of our situation is that we are, like it or not, in an invisible world; and therefore it remains to you to make a respectful petition to the world of shadows.' 'But is there such a thing?' someone wonders. By adding a 'fourth dimension' to reality, Bely has the make-believe become all-too-real, all-too-suggestive for us today. Three dimensions are too narrow, too restricted. The fourth dimension is the realm of obscurity, the zone of amateur politics. It isn't marked on maps, 'except as a dot, for a dot is the place where the plane of this existence touches against the spherical surface of the immense astral cosmos'.

In Ancient Greece, shadows were seen as falsehoods, in a realm inferior to light; true knowledge was enlightenment, was sunshine. In Plato's famous parable of the cave, underground people chained up, staring at their own shadows before them, with the fire behind, knew nothing of the truth, neither the truth of themselves nor of their world.[13] The truth lay outside the cave, in broad daylight. Shadows, Plato said, are 'manufactured articles', representations of reality, not reality itself. The true isn't your shadow or any 'foolish phantom', it's your real, unreflected self. The problem, said Plato, is that if underground people are released from their cave-prison, will they be able to stand the glare of the truth? Will sunshine make their eyes ache? On the other hand, once adjusted to the light, will they ever be able to return to their undergrounds again, will they still be able to see in the dark?

In the Romantic period, shadows took on a more ambiguous meaning; they were a twilight zone of both truth and falsity, of protection and provocation, of defence and solitude. In the early 1800s, Adelbert von Chamisso wrote a book originally for children in praise of shadows. In *Peter Schlemihl*, von Chamisso introduces a nameless Underground Man who sells his shadow to a 'man in grey' – we might have said, to a man in a grey suit. ('Schlemihl', from Yiddish, denotes an unlucky person, a loser whose ventures invariably turn out badly. It's gallows humour right out of Baudelaire and Dostoevsky.)

Peter Schlemihl is von Chamisso's version of the Faust legend, and the man in grey is the devil himself. In exchange for his shadow, our anti-hero receives bags of gold, infinite riches that enable him to go anywhere and do anything he likes. At first he's jubilant. His social standing goes up, he's no longer a loser, an outsider; he's a 'sir', even a 'count'. At one point he's mistaken for the king of Prussia, and people bow down in his honour. But after a while, Schlemihl begins to realise that something is deeply lacking; he feels only half a man. He has no past, no background, no connections – he's stunningly rich yet somehow deficient, without a soul. He has sold part of his own identity to a mysterious stranger, who's given him untold wealth. And yet with the arrival of this wealth, something has gone, something has been taken away from his interior.

Soon, he yearns for his shadow back. He wants to be whole again. He regrets selling it over in the first place and hopes it's not too late to redeem himself, to save himself. He possesses treasures but his life is no longer worth living. *Peter Schlemihl* is a tale of somebody who thinks they're seeing the light – attaining the spotlight, even grabbing the limelight – so they willingly mutilate themselves to get it. If you get rid of your shadow, you'll see the light. You'll know the truth about yourself. Plato would have agreed, but von Chamisso begs to differ; as does Bely, as would Dostoevsky and Baudelaire. 'Remember, my friend,' says von Chamisso at the end of his tale, 'while you live in this world, treasure your shadow.'[14] We need to keep hold of our darker side to nourish ourselves: it must never be sold to any professional.

We've seen this shadow citizenry step out of the shadows in more recent times, into the bright light of day, into the public squares and streets. They've expressed themselves as shadow citizens of the world, gathering in crowds, yet always dispersing again. Where are they now? Underground again, for the time being – perhaps back inside their caves. One of Arendt's central claims in *The Human Condition* is that all effective politics takes place in the light, in the visible public realm – in what she calls 'the space of appearance'. I think this is only partly true – a half-truth, if you will. I think the amateur spirit is more shadowy, more clandestine, more protective. It should be the haunting of the mainstream. It may never actually be the mainstream.

Somehow, Arendt's 'space of appearance' doesn't seem quite right. Indeed, the politics of the shadow citizenry isn't defined only by appearance but also by opacity and anonymity, by clandestinity and dissimulation, by invisibility, all of which can be unnerving for the powers that be. The power of surprise, of secret organisation, of rebelling and plotting covertly, of striking unpredictably and in multiple sites at once, is one way in which relatively weak collectivities of people can confront a professional power whose arsenal is vastly superior. To appear visibly and explicitly – in a manoeuvre, in organising, in an occupation – is to be exposed, and thus vulnerable.

Over the past decade, we've witnessed black ski caps and Guy Fawkes masks become emblems of radical politics, guises of veritable amateur nobodies, of anonymous underground men and women, superfluous people without apparent qualities who want to disguise their own inner qualities. These people shun visibility in public and have little desire to be the somebody the professional world wants them to be. They are expressive bodies, yet they're also bodies weary of revealing too much of themselves, which is why they may adopt disguises and masks: bodies reveal their true identities by dissimulating their faces, altering themselves, transgressing how they're supposed to act and look.

How can a shadow citizenry affirm its collective identity, its collective vitality, its collective coming together and staying together? How can a shadow citizenry encounter and bond with one another? How can they do it both in public and in secret, in daylight and in the shadows? What new arenas could promote shadow citizen bonding and the collective assembly of amateur

shadow citizens? Is it possible to conceive of new shadow institutions that might affirm rank amateurism? Can we think of new
forms of trust and exchange, new systems of communication, new
amateur spaces? These might be alternatives in which amateur
populations can affirm themselves in the shorter term, while building up more robust oppositional capacities over the longer term.

For the Ancient Greeks, the great arena was the agora, the public
space where Athenians gathered and debated politics, debated
democracy. Maybe what is needed now, as our democracy is put up
for tender, is some kind of new citizens' agora – a *shadow citizens'
agora* – a place where a phantom amateur public might constitute
a solid citizenry, a revolutionary citizenry. Like the agora of old,
this would be a stage for tragic drama, where a shadow citizens'
catharsis is enacted. A forum where shadow citizens can engage in
epic theatre, where they can debate and argue, analyse and rectify
their democratic lack.

But the shadow citizens' agora must be something more than the
hijacked public spaces we have nowadays, those Privately Owned
Public Spaces (POPS) and branded plazas that have somehow
branded us. We can do better, a lot better, ourselves. We need to
invent another public realm, defined by participating amateurs
affirming a general will; a place where left-handers can challenge
right-handers, and where, in the short term at least, fellow-
travellers can discuss collective hopes and collective fears, and
work them through together.

For that, we need new clubs and societies, meeting halls and
debating chambers, cafés and social clubs, youth centres and
off-campus 'deschooled' classrooms (like the 'University of
Orange' in New Jersey, an open, volunteer-taught project, with
its own, orange, shadow passport).[15] We need places and spaces
where 'general assemblies' might be forged and where people can

congregate non-commercially, encountering other people actively. Because, let's face it, there's a dearth of spaces where people can engage with one another on a human scale, face-to-face; it's hard to find someplace that isn't about shopping or gawping and doesn't involve having some digital screen shoved in your face. It's hard to turn the sound down, stop the music, ignore the ads, and *talk*. Shadow citizens' agoras need to ensure that hitherto-silenced people have a voice, get a word in edgeways, are heard, and sometimes challenged.

But to speak out in public, as a public searching for democratic consensus, there's a need for a free press, an alternative underground media including independent free radio – something like *Radio Alice*, 'Red' Bologna's politically aligned pirate station from the mid-1970s, which mixed autonomous labour protests and political analyses with recipes and yoga lessons. An independent free media might be developed along the lines of Raymond Williams's great vision from *Communications*, in which he hatches a 'Proposal' for socialist arts and media channels, neither profit-orientated nor state-controlled; managed by, and expressive of, democratically elected bodies.

In TV, Williams says, 'the means of production and transmission could be publicly owned but vested in several independent trusts.' The BBC, he says, has an excellent reputation of 'public service broadcasting', but it equally 'exemplifies the dangers of a very large organisation, in which producers become subject to administrators'. The huge concentration of power in the press will take a while to remedy, but 'the first step should be to free local newspapers from the remote control of financial empires', Williams says. 'A Local Newspaper Trust, in which working editors and journalists would have a majority, could be publicly financed to regain ownership. Local trusts could be organised to guarantee the independence of editors, with the right to appeal to the national body.'[16]

My tatty, second-hand Penguin copy of Williams's *Communications* is revealing of our times in another, ironic way. On its front cover there's a long blurb, emblazoned in vivid purple, calling it 'A most valuable book for anyone concerned with the state of the chief means of communication in this country – television, films, theatre, advertising, books and magazines'. On the inside flap, however, a large official stamp appears: 'WITHDRAWN'. Nothing else: it doesn't say from which public library or university *Communications* was withdrawn, or in which year, but the official-dom of the announcement, in upper case, is unsettling. It could have easily come out of Orwell's *1984*, or *V for Vendetta*, as the censorship of a totalitarian state rather too close to home, a state that doesn't want its citizens reading 'valuable books' about 'the state of the chief means of communication in this country'.

Williams envisions a genuine free media, maybe we could say an 'amateur media', open and publicly accessible, which nowadays would be online as well as in print.[17] It would include a local and national press that reports on ideas and news items people might want to hear about, not the celebrity gossip and right-wing pro-paganda that mainstream monopoly media and broadcast services boom out every hour, the fear and loathing peddled by News International and Fox, or the reactionary tabloid sound bites of the *Daily Mail*. Real news and experimental arts, news and arts from other sources, news and ideas and truths that usually don't get a look-in, that aren't allowed to be heard – they need to be channelled and disseminated.

Speaking out requires forums in which shadow citizens can come together en masse. Democracy must allow people to assemble, peaceably, without arms; though if this 'right' is denied, if the principles of free assembly are opposed, then the sub-clause is that citizens ought to be able to assemble through any means necessary, peaceable or otherwise. It's in the resulting agora that shadow citizens have the power to act, to act after being heard, after having listened to others. It's in the shadow citizens' agora that people can assert themselves as citizens of a participatory democracy. Is there a role for architects and engineers in helping create these new agoras as social spaces? Is there a role for utopian architects and engineers, for activist architects and engineers who might act like real amateurs, putting their specialisms to better use in the exploration of *weak* architecture, an architecture of the anti-spectacle, an architecture of radical social human space – not of glitzy commercial physical space?

The design critic Justin McGuirk recently got inspired by radical happenings in Latin America and uses this experience to set out an 'activist architect's methodology'. 'It is not about [creating] passive forms', says McGuirk, 'but active forms: systems, networks, connections, infrastructure.'[18] This is not an architecture of elitist professional celebration, but one that creates the conditions for action to occur, action that connects ordinary people, that hooks people up together and helps install new, radical sorts of infrastructure that amateurs can't provide by themselves. In activist architecture, the urban isn't so much a *tabula rasa* as a potential *terra nova*, rooted in old land, in its rubble.

And it isn't high-tech urban design that's at stake, either; more a matter of low-budget *urban acupuncture*, of finding new amateurish ways to recreate old stuff, of poking into things meticulously and lovingly to enable sociability – not rolling in roughshod with the professional bulldozer. 'To work in the community's interests', McGuirk notes, 'you need the citizens on your side, because the days of telling people what's good for them are over.' At least they should be. Acupuncture only makes sense, he quotes a colleague as saying, if there's a body, and 'the city is the body. In other words, micro-projects only have a significant impact beyond their immediate site if they are part of a network of actions across the city.'

That's what's meant by *weak* architecture: it's the opposite of erecting *strong* buildings, of designing and constructing to impress. It's about nurturing activities in the interstices of those immense buildings, particularly communal activities, collective amateur activities, maybe even collective amateur political activities. It's more about nurturing street space, developing floor space, re-energising vacant lots and dormant plazas, subverting what's within those spectacular projects, those Shards and Guggenheims, those Le Corbusier masterworks, what's within and under the stilts and pillars in the sky. It's about shaking up the very foundations upon which strong buildings are built.

That's the strength of weak architecture. Weak architecture tackles the paradox of designing spontaneity, the paradox of dealing with paradox. And we're not talking here about professional architects like Robert Venturi simply pandering to pop culture. It's a matter of creating the ingredients that Lefebvre saw as necessary for spaces to palpitate, to live and breathe, to be politicised – proximity and union, assembly and encounter, co-presence and difference. All great stuff, great meaningful stuff for amateurs: a value system pitched at street level, at amateur walk-up level.

The essential thing is to construct a human space in which sensual and experiential communication can be most effectively transmitted. Physicality morphs into sociality. What is abstractly conceived can function only insofar as it infiltrates the lived, only insofar as it becomes a shared and agreed-upon reality. Here, being mutually aware of how we are simultaneously participants and spectators in our collective destiny has obvious political ramifications. Guy Debord said that the more we contemplate life as spectators, the less we live it. The more we behave as passive objects in our society and culture, the less we actively participate in the production of our own life. Then, things will be done *to* us rather than *by* us. Our own ability to realise ourselves, to affirm ourselves, will be significantly stunted and stultified. Other people, people who reign over us, who perform *for* us, who represent us, barely dialoguing with us, will draft the script of our life.

Debord and Lefebvre both opposed role-playing in all forms of social custom. They opposed amateurs playing roles as professionals, being forced into becoming wannabe professionals. What we're talking about here is a new, self-scripted value system; not about professional jargon but about *vernacular values* spoken at source, spoken truthfully, embodied in space and architecture, a value system more expressive of how people really *feel*, what they want, what they need, and how they might get it. Vernacular values are more inclusive language-games, the mutterings of a post-professional ethos, of a new social imaginary.

There are no standard passports for spiritual citizens of the universe, no passports for those who know they live someplace yet feel they belong everyplace. This conjoining of knowing and feeling, of experience close and experience wide, is what engenders a sense of empathy whose *nom de plume* might really be citizenship itself, authenticated by the shadow passport that's inside you. It's an 'imagined community', but one of a global imagination. Here, we might take 'dwelling' in its broadest existential sense, of being the centre of one's own life: dwelling is the totality of political and developmental space in which you feel you belong. Citizenship grows as an affinity between shadowy selves who become aware of one another as a shadow citizenry struggling within a bigger underground reality, one of actuality and possibility.

If this shadow citizenry were to cast itself around the European continent today, we might see how the connections between, say, Athens and Frankfurt, Lisbon and London, Berlin and Paris, Amsterdam and Brussels, Marseille and Madrid, Barcelona and Milan, Rome and Bucharest, Vienna and Budapest, Dublin and Liverpool, Krakow and Hamburg, all stack up, all coexist, as the warp and woof of what Europe is, of what an alternative European community might be, a shadow Europe. It's a threading that entangles everyone, that stitches together a patchwork continental cloth. But imagine if we could get amateur delegates from the grassroots of all these cities together, in one great big European citizens' agora, with those shadow people working in communities, people organising and strategising, envisioning experimental projects and concrete utopias. Imagine if we got them to put their imaginations and know-hows together, had them debating and collaborating in this new agora, talking openly and frankly about the issues that are important to the shadow citizenry: about citizenship and rights to the city, about free time rather than mindless work time, about creative amateur self-expression and Hobby-Horsical activities … We might expect such a dialogue and wish-list to be very different from the professional spiel we hear today in Brussels.

First off, we'd grant austerity drives only insofar as they apply to the downsizing and planned shrinkage of the over-paid, tax-dodging bureaucratic and financial sector, much of which lobbies and manages the European Commission administration. These 'belt-tightening' initiatives, laying off public-private bankers and bureaucrats whom nobody would miss anyway, would free up considerable sums of 'obscure resources' for affordable housing strategies; a lot of European citizens would find this attractive and necessary. We've already got an array of radical housing networks across Europe, whose agendas could be better coordinated and more robustly consolidated with increased financing. We might shut down the European Central Bank and replace it with its other, with the shadow citizens' other – a real shadow banking programme called the European Central Community Bank (ECCB), managed by democratically elected participants from a host of European cities, 'councillors' who would ensure that representation doesn't move away from everyday life.

A group of 'Scrutineers' would oversee these councillors' operations and act as a Governing Body belonging to a 'Nocturnal Council' (Plato's idea), again comprising amateur, elected, shadow volunteers, whose tenure would rotate every two years. With ECCB backing, we might see the instigation of 'Community Land Trusts', collectively owned land and property foundations which would create another notion of the public realm, one not owned and managed by any centralised state but by a collective of people, federated and communal, truly responsive to citizens' needs.

Community Land Trusts would curb property speculation and help incubate economic and cultural activities around local community use-values rather than privately plundered exchange-values, devising innovative transport strategies along the way, while limiting car usage. They'd experiment with renewable energies and mass transit schemes, and promote biking and green-space development in the office nodes of old. Grass-carpeted 'High Lines' might meander through the former financial wildernesses of Canary Wharf and make central Brussels less bleak because its EU bureaucratic citadel would be no more.

Meanwhile, with large-scale bureaucratic downscaling of the parasitic professional elite, we might then develop initiatives to bolster 'happy unemployment', providing an unconditional and guaranteed income to people without jobs. They will now have time on their hands to do more useful and rewarding 'tasks', tasks that can re-energise their communities and themselves, tasks performed on a strictly non-commercial basis. Here we'll glimpse our shadow economic system, perhaps a Local Exchange Trading System (LETS), in which ex-professionals might want to get involved, too, joining the ranks of the 'happy unemployed'. They might become new people, with amateur outlooks. 'Open money' might enter into this trading system, money that doesn't accumulate value, doesn't beget more money and capital. Now, it's money that's simply a token of relative worth of the goods and services swapped.

This kind of money could be the basis of interest-free credit. We might imagine a situation in which local people can trade goods and services in kind, with the ability to issue money themselves – a local currency that serves their own needs, that finances community undertakings. With regard to larger projects, or bigger, more elaborate infrastructure, communities would approach the ECCB, not only for the wherewithal but also for a knowledge base and 'specialist' advice – freely and independently given, of course. Under this paradigm, a vernacular value system would inspire a process of 'convivial reconstruction' (as Ivan Illich put it). In this new, convivial Europe, science and technique would be at the service of more effective 'use-value' generation, used to invent and realise social infrastructure, unmeasured and indeed unmeasurable by professional need-creators.

Something wonderful might likewise happen to the shadow citizens of this convivial society. People's sense of individuality and self-worth might change. When you looked into the mirror, you'd no longer see somebody who sells themselves to the highest bidder. No more need to carve up your personality and join the ranks of the bad-faith professional classes or unhappy employed. You might become the person you once wanted to be before you sold out your value system, cashed in your identity in order to play a phoney game. What we might glimpse once these fetters have gone is the release of a process of self-recovery.

You might see a new person blossom, energised and illuminated, a person who flourishes through this process of self-discovery, who's busy being born again. And unlike Leopold Bloom from Joyce's *Ulysses* – who tried to write in the sand the person he was but couldn't quite muster the courage to say it, to continue the phrase, 'I AM A ...' – now you can erase the ellipsis, fill in the blanks yourself, finish Bloom's job, *bloom*, and affirm your authentic self. Because this, in the end, or at the start of a new beginning, is what amateurism is really all about.

Acknowledgements

I owe an enormous debt to Leo Hollis at Verso for his unwavering support for this project. He went through the text painstakingly, line by line, and made helpful suggestions to shape up the form and content of what eventually appeared in print, often having a better sense of what I was trying to do than I did myself. Meanwhile, none of it would have ever been possible without Corinna and Lili-Rose, my beloved wife and daughter, to whom this book is dedicated.

Notes

Preface

1 Fyodor Dostoevsky, *Notes from Underground* [1864], trans. Boris Jakim (William B. Eerdmans Publishing, Grand Rapids, Michigan, 2009), Part 2, Section III, p. 62.

1. Professionals and Amateurs

1 Marshall Berman, *All That Is Solid Melts into Air: The Experience of Modernity* (Simon and Schuster, New York, 1982); see Chapter 1, 'Goethe's *Faust*: The Tragedy of Development'.

2 Quoted in Berman, *All That Is Solid Melts into Air*, p. 67.

3 Joe Flood, *The Fires: How a Computer Formula, Big Ideas, and the Best of Intentions Burned Down New York City – and Determined the Future of Cities* (Riverhead, New York, 2010).

4 Roger Starr, *Urban Choices: The City and Its Critics* (Penguin, Harmondsworth, 1967). Starr's coinage of 'Planned Shrinkage' came a little later, in 'Making New York Smaller', *New York Times Magazine*, 14 November 1976.

5 Starr, *Urban Choices*, p. 41.

6 Starr, *Urban Choices*, p. 23.

7 Jane Jacobs, *Death and Life of Great American Cities* (Penguin, Harmondsworth, 1961), p. 437.

8 Crucially, by 1981 much of Toxteth had already been devastated by

professional urban renewal initiatives. Like sections of the South Bronx, areas had been completely abandoned and stripped of people and services. Hence part of the rationale behind the rioting.

9 'Toxteth Riots: Howe Proposed "Managed Decline" for City', *BBC News*, 30 December 2011, bbc.co.uk.

10 Said's Reith lectures are published in an invaluable little book called *Representations of the Intellectual* (Vintage Books, New York, 1994); Chapter 4 deals explicitly with 'Professionals and Amateurs'. His thesis can still be heard orally, in all its eloquent glory, on the Radio 4 website: bbc.co.uk/programmes.

11 Said, *Representations of the Intellectual*, p. 51.

12 Said, *Representations of the Intellectual*, p. 57.

2. A Question of Faith

1 Blaise Pascal, *Pensées*, Section IV, 'Of the Means of Belief', #252.

2 'Public Bodies (Reform) Bill', 23 May 2010: gov.uk/government/speeches.

3 See David Boyle, 'Target Culture: Back from the Dead', *Guardian*, 8 October 2010.

4 James C. Scott, *Seeing Like a State: How Certain Schemes to Improve the Human Condition Have Failed* (Yale University Press, New Haven, 1998), p. 12. Scott, a retired political scientist-cum-anthropologist, is also an anarchist who doesn't believe the state will ever be abolished. 'It's a matter of taming the state', he says.

5 Scott, *Seeing Like a State*, p. 15.

6 Edmund Wilson, *The Cold War and the Income Tax: A Protest* (W. H. Allen, London, 1964). Nowadays, too, the poor are milked for taxes while the rich get off scot-free or almost. Similarly, Britain's nuclear defence system, Trident, guzzles more than £30 billion annually; after the 2008 financial crisis, Royal Bank of Scotland received £45 billion of taxpayers' money, Lloyds £20 billion.

7 Wilson, *The Cold War and the Income Tax*, p. 41.

8 David Foster Wallace, *The Pale King* (Little, Brown and Company, New York, 2011), p. 548.

9 Foster Wallace, *The Pale King*, p. 85.

10 Foster Wallace, *The Pale King*, p. 87.

11 Foster Wallace, *The Pale King*, p. 548.

12 David Graeber, *The Utopia of Rules: On Technology, Stupidity, and the Secret Joys of Bureaucracy* (Melville House, New York, 2015), pp. 5–6.

13 Franz Kafka, *The Trial* (Modern Library Edition, New York, 1964), p. 6.

14 Franz Kafka, *The Castle* (Penguin, London, 1997), p. 53.

15 See Reiner Stach, *Kafka: The Decisive Years* (Princeton University Press, Princeton, 2005), especially Chapter 21.

16 Kafka, *The Trial*, pp. 262–3.

17 Kafka, *The Castle*, p. 52.

18 Max Weber, 'The End of Capitalism?' in Stanislav Andreski, ed., *Max Weber on Capitalism, Bureaucracy and Religion: A Selection of Texts* (George Allen & Unwin, London, 1983), p. 159.

19 Karl Marx, *Critique of Hegel's Philosophy of Right*. See Part III on 'The Executive', especially 'Addition to Section 297': marxists.org/archive.

20 Fyodor Dostoevsky, *Notes from Underground* [1864], trans. Boris Jakim (William B. Eerdmans Publishing, Grand Rapids, Michigan, 2009), p. 24.

21 N.G.Chernyshevsky, *What Is To Be Done?* (Virago Press, London, 1982), pp. 319–20.

3. *The Measure of Knowledge*

1 Karl Marx, *Capital*, *Volume One* (Penguin, Harmondsworth, 1976), Chapter IX, Section 3, p. 333.

2 Robert Pollin, Michael Ash and Thomas Herndon, 'Does High Public Debt Consistently Stifle Economic Growth? A Critique of Reinhart and Rogoff' (University of Massachusetts Amherst, Political Economy Research Institute Working Paper #322, April 2013); see also Robert Pollin and Michael Ash, 'Debt and Growth: A Response to Reinhart and Rogoff', *New York Times*, Op-Ed, 29 April 2013.

3 Viktor Mayer-Schönberger and Kenneth Cukier, *Big Data: A Revolution That Will Transform How We Live, Work, and Think* (John Murray Publishers, London, 2013).

4 See Chris Anderson, 'The End of Theory: The Data Deluge Makes the Scientific Method Obsolete', *Wired Magazine*, 23 June 2008.

5 Andrew McAfee and Erik Brynjolfsson, 'Big Data: The Management Revolution', *Harvard Business Review*, October 2012. Incidentally, MIT Media Lab's list of sponsors include: Toshiba, Samsung, Panasonic, 21st Century Fox, Colgate-Palmolive and Coca-Cola, to name only a handful out of a whole host of multi-nationals.

6 MOOCs are e-boosted distance learning platforms with unlimited educational participation and open access teaching. Everything is posted online, and students interact with professors via 'user forums'. There's much that is positive about MOOCs. But it's a growth industry as well. For-profit service providers jockey with non-profit foundations for market dominance and educational patents. For cash-strapped universities, it's a smart means to provide educational structure without any educational infrastructure. And this ostensibly 'free' education espouses a business model: degree accreditation frequently comes at a price.

7 'The Metric Tide: Report of the Independent Review of the Role of Metrics in Research Assessment and Management', July 2015, Higher Education Funding Council for England.

8 Ivan Illich, *Deschooling Society* (Penguin, Harmondsworth, 1973), p. 72. Illich, who died in 2002 at the age of seventy-six, was an Austrian by birth, a Jew who became a Catholic, a priest who denounced the Vatican, a global intellectual who toured continents on foot; a Marxist who castigated Marxism, a socialist against welfarism, he lived a rich life as an ascetic.

9 'Fulfilling Our Potential', gov.uk/government/consultations.

10 See the *Times Higher Education* 'University Workplace Survey 2016: results and analysis', timeshighereducation.com.

4. *City of Amateurs*

1 Walter Benjamin, 'Unpacking My Library', in *Illuminations* (Schocken Books, New York, 1968), p. 63.

2 Cited in 'Notes on *Pull My Daisy*', in Jack Sargeant, *Naked Lens: Beat Cinema* (Creation Books, London, 1997), p. 19. The Swiss-born Robert Frank came to the US in 1948; *The Americans* (Scalo Publishers, Zurich, 1998), first published in France in 1958, is a roving series of realist images seen through an outsider lens.

3 Jane Jacobs, *Death and Life of Great American Cities* (Penguin, Harmondsworth, 1961), pp. 60–1.

4 Jacobs, *Death and Life of Great American Cities*, pp. 62–3.

5 Jacobs's article is available online as part of *Fortune*'s Greatest Hits series: fortune.com/2011/09/18.

6 William H. Whyte, *The Social Life of Small Urban Spaces* (Project for Public Spaces, New York, 1980).

7 Whyte's Street Life Project made its own *Pull My Daisy*, a splendidly home-baked hour-long documentary from 1979, beautifully evoking amateur wisdom, right down to Whyte's avuncular commentary: archive.org/details/SmallUrbanSpaces#.

8 Edward Glaeser, *Triumph of the City: How Our Greatest Invention Makes Us Richer, Smarter, Greener, Healthier, and Happier* (Penguin, New York, 2011).

9 Richard Florida, *The Rise of the Creative Class: And How It's Transforming Work, Leisure, Community, and Everyday Life* (Basic Books, New York, 2002). Over the past decade Florida has reworked his creative class concept: see *Who's Your City?* (Basic Books, New York, 2008); *The Flight of the Creative Class* (HarperCollins, New York, 2005); *Cities and the Creative Class* (Routledge, New York, 2005).

10 Richard Florida, 'How Zoning Restrictions Make Segregation Worse', *Atlantic*, 4 January 2016. Florida can write any nonsense he likes in the *Atlantic* magazine, because he's a senior editor there.

11 Jane Jacobs, 'Downtown Is for People', *Fortune Magazine*, April 1958.

12 In 2009, Tony Hsieh, CEO of the online start-up fashion company Zappos, invested $200 million of his own money in fifty-five acres of downtown Las Vegas to build the 'co-working capital of the world', an entrepreneurial high-tech nirvana. But as urban critic Leo Hollis objected: 'The city is not a start-up. It is not a market … The city is not a platform that can be hacked. Despite the optimistic talk, it is an old language that is spoken here: start-up urbanism is gentrification by another name.' See Leo Hollis, 'Why Start-up Urbanism Will Fail Us', shareable.net.

13 See lsecities.net.

14 See bsigroup.com.

15 Fyodor Dostoevsky, *Notes from Underground* [1864], trans. Boris Jakin (William B. Eerdmans Publishing, Grand Rapids, Michigan, 2009), p. 24.

16 Dostoevsky, *Notes from Underground*, p. 51.

17 Bookchin's oeuvre on anarchism, politics and ecology is prodigious. For an insight into his urban thinking, see *The Limits of the City* (Black Rose Books, Montreal, 1986); *Urbanization without Cities* (Black Rose Books, Montreal, 1992); *From Urbanisation to Cities* (Cassell, London, 1995); and, more recently, *The Next Revolution* (Verso, London, 2015).

18 Murray Bookchin, *From Urbanisation to Cities*, p. 64.

19 These quotations come from Debord's 1978 film, *In Girum Imus Nocte et Consumimur Igni*. For a transcript, see Guy Debord, *Œuvres* (Gallimard, Paris, 2006), pp. 1334–420. The title is a Latin palindrome: 'We go around and around in the night and are consumed by fire.'

20 Guy Debord, *Panegyric* (Verso, London, 1991), p. 12.

21 Debord, *Panegyric*, p. 21.

22 Debord, *Panegyric*, p. 39. Like Debord, Chevalier saw the destruction of Les Halles' old market halls, begun in February 1969, as a terminal violation of Paris. There was hardly anyone to contemplate the scene, he recalled, save 'a few nocturnal creatures, a few nostalgia seekers, a few poets, a few clochards'. Louis Chevalier,

The Assassination of Paris (Chicago University Press, Chicago, 1994).

5. *Work in the Crystal Palace*

1 Robert Neuwirth, *The Stealth of Nations: The Global Rise of the Informal Economy* (Pantheon, New York, 2011), p. 179.

2 'New "Gig" Economy Spells End of Lifetime Careers', *Financial Times*, 5 August 2015.

3 Alan Harrington, *Life at the Crystal Palace* (Alfred Knopf, New York, 1959).

4 Dave Eggers, *The Circle* (Penguin, London, 2013).

5 For a fascinating insight into historical changes in workspace design, see Nikil Saval's *Cubed: A Secret History of the Workplace* (Doubleday, New York, 2014).

6 William Davies, *The Happiness Industry: How the Government and Big Business Sold Us Well-Being* (Verso, London, 2015), p. 113.

7 'What's Causing Zappos to "Hemorrhage" Talent?' *Forbes Magazine*, 7 April 2016; see also 'The Zappos Exodus Continues After a Radical Management Experiment', *New York Times*, 13 January 2016.

8 See 'Congratulations! You've Been Fired', *New York Times*, 9 April 2016.

9 'Congratulations! You've been Fired'.

10 Davies, *The Happiness Industry*, p. 106.

11 Guillaume Paoli, *Éloge de la démotivation* [*In Praise of Demotivation*] (Éditions Lignes, Fécamp, 2008). Paoli (b. 1959) is a German who writes in French, a freelance writer, philosopher and journalist who's also worked in theatre.

12 Herman Melville, *Bartleby* (Dover Publications, New York, 1990), p. 21.

13 Lautréamont, *Maldoror and Poésies* (Penguin, London, 1978), p. 280. Lautréamont died, aged twenty-four, of a fever during the siege of Paris in the Franco-Prussian War. Part II of *Poésies* 'rerouted' a host of famous verses and maxims from classic authors.

Debord compared the 'irrevocable brilliance' of *Poésies* to almost being struck by lightning in his garden (*Panegyric*, p. 42).

14 Guillaume Paoli et le Collectif, *Manifeste des chômeurs heureux* (Éditions Libertalia, Paris, 2013), p. 31.

15 Paoli, *Manifeste des chômeurs heureux*, p. 57.

16 André Gorz, *Bâtir la civilisation du temps libre* (Éditions Les liens qui libèrent, Paris, 2013), p. 57.

17 See 'Your Job Title is ... What?' *New York Times*, 25 October 2015.

18 Jean-Paul Sartre, *Being and Nothingness* (Washington Square Press, New York, 1956), p. 87.

19 See Sartre, *Being and Nothingness*, pp. 101–3.

20 Harrington, *Life in the Crystal Palace*, p. 143.

21 Harrington, *Life in the Crystal Palace*, p. 149.

6. *Professional Democracy*

1 Guy Debord, *Comments on the Society of the Spectacle* (Verso, London, 1990), p. 21.

2 Simon Cox, 'The Accountant Kings', *File on 4*, BBC Radio 4, 4 March 2014, transcript.

3 Pierre Bourdieu, 'The Left Hand and the Right Hand of the State', in Bourdieu, *Acts of Resistance: Against the Tyranny of the Market* (Monthly Review Press, New York, 1998).

4 Pierre Bourdieu, *Sur l'état: Cours au Collège de France, 1989–1992* (Éditions du Seuil, Paris, 2012).

5 Bourdieu, *Sur l'état*, p42.

6 There is a fascinating 2001 documentary on Bourdieu by Pierre Carles, *La sociologie est un sport de combat* [*Sociology Is a Martial Art*]. Edward Said also appears, introducing a terrified Bourdieu – having to speak in English! – via video transmission to listeners at a New York conference.

7 Bourdieu, 'Against the Destruction of Civilisation', Remarks at the Gare de Lyon, December 1995, in *Acts of Resistance*, pp. 24–8.

8 'Franz Kafka: On the Tenth Anniversary of His Death', in *Illuminations* (Schocken Books, New York, 1968), pp. 111–140.

9 Plato, *The Laws*, Book XII (Penguin, Harmondsworth, 1970), p. 493. The relevant section is entitled 'The Need for Scrutineers'.

10 See Ray Pahl, *Whose City?* (Penguin, Harmondsworth, 1970).

11 John Gittelsohn, 'Fannie Mae Chicago Foreclosures Sell for $11.8 Million', *Bloomberg News*, 2 October 2012, cogsvillegroup.com.

12 During his presidential campaign, the *New Yorker* (12 October 2015) did a profile of Bernie Sanders, 'The Populist Prophet', highlighting how his 'gruffness, didacticism, and indifference to appearances ... are central to his appeal. All his friends described Sanders as "authentic", a word that many people would be hesitant to apply to Hillary Clinton.'

13 'Revealed: How Jeremy Corbyn has Reshaped the Labour Party', *Guardian*, 13 January 2016.

14 Tara Conlan, 'Has Jeremy Corbyn Changed the Art of Political Interviewing?' *Guardian*, 4 October 2015. For a deeper look into how Corbyn is dishonestly represented by the British media – particularly by the BBC – see Paul Myerscough, 'Corbyn in the Media', *London Review of Books*, 22 October 2015.

15 Hilary Wainwright, *The Tragedy of the Private, The Potential of the Public* (Transnational Institute, Amsterdam, 2014), p. 31.

7. The Genius of Curiosity

1 Charles Baudelaire, 'The Painter of Modern Life', in Baudelaire, *Selected Writings on Art and Literature* (Penguin, Harmondsworth, 1972), p. 395.

2 Constantin Guys (1805–1892) was a painter, engraver and draughtsman of Flemish origin. For a while he travelled as a correspondent for the *Illustrated London News*. Baudelaire recognised Guys' amateur genius for representing what is eternal and contingent in the modern world.

3 Baudelaire, 'The Painter of Modern Life', p. 397.

4 Walter Benjamin, *Charles Baudelaire: A Lyric Poet in the Era of High Capitalism* (Verso, London, 1973).

5 Charles Baudelaire, *Comment on paie ses dettes quand on a du génie* (Flammarion, Paris, 2015).

6 Baudelaire, 'The Painter of Modern Life', p. 402.

7 'Enivrez-Vous' [Intoxicate Yourself], is one of Baudelaire's *Spleen de Paris* prose poems, from 1864. The translation here is my own.

8 Baudelaire, 'The Painter of Modern Life', p. 398.

9 Baudelaire, 'The Painter of Modern Life', p. 400.

10 Baudelaire, 'The Painter of Modern Life', p. 400.

11 Charles Baudelaire, 'The Heroism of Modern Life', in Baudelaire, *Selected Writings*, p. 106.

12 Charles Baudelaire, 'The Salon of 1859' in Baudelaire, *Art in Paris, 1845–1862: Reviews of Salons & Other Exhibitions* (Phaidon, London, 1965), p. 155.

13 Baudelaire, 'The Salon of 1859', p. 156.

14 Baudelaire, 'The Salon of 1859', p. 162.

15 For a more elaborate discussion of the idea of 'intensity' in both Baudelaire and Dostoevsky, see Alex de Jonge's *Dostoevsky and the Age of Intensity* (Secker & Warburg, London, 1975). Part I is devoted to 'Baudelaire and the Romantic Heritage'.

16 Baudelaire, lines from 'The Sun' and 'The Enemy', in *Les Fleurs du mal*, cited in Walter Benjamin, *The Writer of Modern Life: Essays on Baudelaire* (Belknap Press of Harvard University Press, Cambridge, MA, 2006).

8. Hobby-Horse

1 Tony Ross, *My Favourite Fairy Tales* (Andersen Press, London, 2010).

2 Laurence Sterne, *The Life and Opinions of Tristram Shandy, Gentleman* (Oxford University Press, Oxford, 1983).

3 Uncle Toby was one of Guy Debord's literary heroes.

4 Andy Merrifield, *The Wisdom of Donkeys* (Walker Books, New York, 2008).

5 Sartre, *Being and Nothingness*, p. 9.

6 The screenplay of this remarkable film is available in book form:

see Wallace Shawn and André Gregory, *My Dinner with André* (Grove Press, New York, 1981).

7 Jerzy Grotowski, *Towards a Poor Theatre* (Clarion Books, New York, 1968).

8 Better said, the 'professional people race'. In another of my favourite books, likewise a children's story, *Mrs. Frisby and the Rats of Nimh* (1971), by Robert O'Brien, the smartest rat, Nicodemus, discovers that 'The Rat Race' 'means a race where, no matter how fast you run, you don't get anywhere. ... I thought, it wasn't a rat race at all, it was a People Race, and no sensible rats would ever do anything so foolish.'

9 Marshall Berman, *The Politics of Authenticity: Radical Individualism and the Emergence of Modern Society* (Atheneum Books, New York, 1970), p. 310.

9. The Amateur Revolution

1 Vladimir I. Lenin, 'What Is to Be Done?' in Robert Tucker, ed., *The Lenin Anthology* (W. W. Norton & Co., New York, 1975), pp. 75–6, with Lenin's emphases.

2 Edmund Wilson, *To the Finland Station* (Doubleday Anchor Books, New York, 1955), p. 384.

3 Here Arendt first aired her thesis on the 'banality of evil', based on Eichmann's role as an instrument of the Nazi 'Final Solution'. For Arendt, Eichmann wasn't a fanatical monster but a high-ranking stiff following orders, a bureaucrat of mediocre intelligence. His evil was the evil of his job description. 'He did his *duty*, as he told the police and the court over and over again; he not only obeyed *orders*, he also obeyed the *law*.' Arendt's report caused outrage in Jewish communities; but the banality of evil lives on, albeit in less genocidal forms.

4 Hannah Arendt, *The Last Interview and Other Conversations* (Melville House, London, 2013).

5 Hannah Arendt, *On Revolution* (Penguin, Harmondsworth, 1963), p. 260.

6 Rachel Carson, *Silent Spring* (Hamish Hamilton, London, 1963).

7 Cited in Jane Jacobs, *The Last Interview and Other Conversations* (Melville House, New York, 2016), p9.

8 Arendt, *On Revolution*, p. 277.

9 Henri Lefebvre, *Le temps des méprises* (Éditions Stock, Paris, 1975), p. 128.

10 Hannah Arendt, *The Human Condition* (University of Chicago Press, Chicago, 1958), p. 198.

11 Henri Lefebvre, 'Quand la ville se perd dans une métamorphose planétaire', *Le Monde diplomatique*, May 1989, p. 17.

12 Andrei Bely, *Petersburg* (Penguin, London, 1995), p. 95.

13 Plato, *The Republic* (Everyman Edition, London, 1935), Book VII.

14 Adelbert von Chamisso, *Peter Schlemihl* (One World Classics, Richmond, 2008), p. 124.

15 Since 2007, the University has been open to everybody for whom 'official' paying universities are firmly shut. Students earn 'Be Free' degrees by taking classes, voting in elections, attending town meetings, and volunteering in the community. Active amateur participation tries to stave off passive professional representation. The University passport is emblazoned with its mascot: Puss in Boots, swashbucklingly dressed, smirking at any border control or Ivy League elite. For more details, see Mindy Fullilove, *Urban Alchemy* (New Village Press, New York, 2013).

16 Raymond Williams, *Communications* (Penguin, Harmondsworth, 1962).

17 In our high-tech internet age, I'd love to think we could reinvent the spirit of the samizdat underground press of the 1960s, full of hard-hitting ideas as well as hard-hitting politics. *Black & Red* comes to mind, founded by Fredy Perlman and his wife Lorraine Nybakken-Perlman. Perlman was a fascinating amateur character himself, an 'unattached intellectual' (in his words) who rejected the academic path. In the 1960s, the Perlmans began a radical education project in Ann Arbor, Michigan. There, they published the

anarchist magazine *Black & Red*, printed off in their living room. They soon expanded into a radical publisher, still around today, whose earliest bestseller was *The Society of the Spectacle*. *Black & Red*'s version of Debord's classic isn't the most accurate translation, yet it's by far the rawest and most revolutionary; with zany graphics, it retains a wonderful sixties shtick. Perlman died way too young, at fifty. His widow's affecting homage, *Having Little, Being Much* (Black & Red Books, Detroit, 1989), is an inspiring epitaph for an amateur life.

18 Justin McGuirk, *Radical Cities: Across Latin America in Search of a New Architecture* (Verso, London, 2014), p. 33.